Cat Massage

Cat Massage

A WHISKERS-TO-TAIL GUIDE
TO YOUR CAT'S ULTIMATE PETTING EXPERIENCE

Maryjean Ballner

ST. MARTIN'S GRIFFIN
New York

Photo credits: Susan Dubal, Patricia Ballner, Maryjean Ballner, Author cover photo: Amjad Ali.

Production Editor: David Stanford Burr
Design: Patrice Sheridan

Library of Congress Cataloging-in-Publication Data

Ballner, Maryjean.
    Cat massage : a whiskers-to-tail guide to your cat's ultimate petting
experience / Maryjean Ballner. —1st ed.
        p. cm.
    ISBN 0-312-15492-5
     1. Cats—Diseases—Alternative treatment.   2. Massage for animals.
I. Title.
SF985.B35   1997
636.8'0895822—dc21   97-7596
                                  CIP

10 9 8 7 6 5 4 3

I dedicate this book to the loving memory of my mother, Florence Siket Ballner, who taught me the beauty of writing and cat loving. And to the loving memory of Bob Arbib, who encouraged me to take a thesis paper and write a book.

On a feline level, I "dedicat" this book to the loving memories of Jingo Neddy, my first cat; Mr. Grey, my first massaging cat; and Piper, Bob Arbib's cat. For lots of cool cats in general, and particularly for the everyday companionship and love of my wonderful cat, Champion.

Acknowledgments

I thank God for the life I have today.

———

Thanks for the support of my entire family, particularly my father, Bill Ballner and my sister Patricia Ballner. To Frank Roff, a dear friend and Bob Weil, who had the keen insight to buy this book when it was a manuscript. To Kathy Burke, for helping me through my toughest times and Linda Raine, for her focused attention and laughter during the complicated moments. To Kim Burkey, a wonderful man from North Dakota who left too soon and too unexpectedly. A special thanks to my friend and Champion's veterinarian, Dr. Andrew Biederman, and my veterinary friend, author and animals rights advocate, Dr. Michael Fox.

Thanks to so many people—you all know how you've helped. And if I forgot your name, be assured I haven't forgotten your kindness. In random order, for their support, laughter, and love, thanks to: Margaret Mazol, Kerrie Flynn, Alan Sommer, Susan Karan, Bob Pollack, Don Amoruso, Rachel Gluckstein, Sandi Font Falcone, Pat and Tony Bono, Tom LoCascio, Marc Grodinsky, Susan McMahon, John Lee, my patient and talented editor Becky Koh, Dr. Scott Torns, Mary and Sal Chiazzese, my aunt, Carolyn Pausic, Bob Bristol, Bob Michaels, Madeline Williams, Bill Maggio, Kim Young, Andy Stavridis, Georgina Webster,

Susan Spina, Glenn Golembiovsky, Suzanne Magida for her expert and talented handiwork, Regina Hopkins Harrison, Walter Keller, Frank Barthel, Mickey Burke, Bill Quaresimo, Dominick Simone and Carl Smith, Herb Goffstein, Scott Meyers, and Joyce Saeger. To Cindy Meyer DVM, Michael Dattner DVM, Heidi Allen DVM, Mitch Beiderman DVM, and Ralphie Concepcion, veterinary technician, who all helped Champion during medical emergency time. And to four very special women: Stacy Bardavid, Liz Bailey, Eileen Abatelli, and Pat Goepfert. To the great background music of Paul Simon, Phoebe Snow, Warren Zevon, Billy Joel, Garth Brooks, Dwight Yoakam, Meatloaf, and Bob Seger ("Deadlines and commitments, what to leave in, what to leave out"). To Peter Mark Roget, Dr. Tadao Ogura and Mary Claps, and the best of the best, Joseph Viik, aka 'Vik.'

Thanks to all the cats I've ever had the pleasure to massage, and especially—Champion, Ground Hog (Bill Ballner), Francesca (Patricia Ballner), Spackle and Noel (Linda Raine), Sheena, Brother, and Sister (Pat and Tony Bono), Kit Kat (Marc and Judy Grodinsky), Delilah (Jan and Jack Pellicano), and Kitty (Rosie and Ryan Thomas).

Contents

Cat Massage

Introduction

Welcome! Your cat will love you for learning Cat Massage. If you've ever enjoyed a professional massage, you know the sublime relaxation this experience brings. Tense, overworked muscles are loosened under the skillful touch of a trained therapist. Flexibility and circulation improve with regular massage. Overall body stress is reduced and stiff, aching joints find relief with therapeutic touch. Massage for people not only feels good, it is good for us. Physicians as well as health and fitness experts around the world promote massage as a valid and essential part of health care.

Since massage is such an important and enjoyable part of our own healthy lifestyle, why shouldn't our cats, who share in all of our other day-to-day activities, also benefit from a regular dose of this touch therapy? In the following pages, you'll discover a comprehensive, easy-to-learn regime of massage therapy for cats—from head to tail!

There is nothing difficult about Cat Massage. As you read through and understand this book, I guarantee that what you will learn is both healthy and enjoyable for your cat. At the same time, your cat will come to trust that your expert touch will give him the ultimate in petting pleasure. Cat Massage contains a repertoire of fifty massage techniques that emphasize every major part of your cat's body.

Most of the strokes concentrate on four key areas—the head, neck, shoulders, and back. When you're comfortable with these, you'll be able to move onto other cat parts, like the belly, tail, and paws. Even some advanced techniques are provided, for when you and your cat are ready for them.

During the process of learning Cat Massage, you're likely to discover certain strokes are more appealing to your cat than others. Try to be particularly sensitive to this. With practice and by recognizing your cat's feedback signals, the two of you will soon create perfect, custom-made massage routines.

Remember, however, that you'll be learning an abundance of information; Cat Massage is an ever-evolving process. Please take your time! Don't feel that you have to learn every technique in one day (or even in one month). There is no rush with Cat Massage. Start off slowly with just one or two massage techniques and build from there. You and your cat will set the pace together.

When I graduated from massage therapy school, I wrote my final paper on cats, entitled "Massage Therapy from a Feline Point of View." During the course of this research, I noticed a distinct change in my Cat, Mr. Grey. Although he had always been affectionate and responsive, something was different. As our petting times became massage sessions, a deeper bond formed between us.

After Mr. Grey went to the big "Cat Club" in the sky, I was heartbroken and cat-less. But soon Champion came to live with me, and I did with Champion what I did with Mr. Grey— Cat Massage. Our friendship transformed into a relationship. I was sure that Cat Massage improved my relationship with Mr. Grey—but I knew it to be the absolute truth with Champion.

I've had years of fun and love with Cat Massage, and you can, too. Just relax, be flexible, be creative, and go for it.

What is Cat Massage?

Cat Massage is a style of petting a cat that generates amazing results. In the dictionary, petting is defined as rubbing. But massage is explained as "rubbing the body for remedial effects." Massage tones muscles, improves circulation, and promotes physical well-being. I upgrade petting—with more detail and finesse—to Cat Massage. When I am no longer randomly rubbing my cat, when I apply specific techniques and motions for desired results, I am doing Cat Massage. And when my cat comes over and demands more petting time, I know I am doing Cat Massage the right way.

As you incorporate my time-tested and cat-approved techniques with your own methods, you will develop the best touch possible for your cat. Rely on your intuition and open yourself to new ideas. Much of Cat Massage is what you know already. This book will help you to do it—only better.

Why Cat Massage?

There are plenty of reasons to massage your cat, and the more you massage, the more you'll see what I mean. In fact, there are dozens of reasons for Cat Massage, some emotional, some psychological, many physical. I'm sure that once you experience its benefits, you'll be looking for any reason to Cat Massage. I know your cat will!

Here are some important reasons to learn Cat Massage:

- It's an all-new way of paying attention to and expressing affection for your cat.
- Routine massage sessions encourage your cat to be more involved with the family (and for your family to be more closely involved with your cat). This is especially good for those who think that cats are too aloof.
- Massage produces an increase in blood circulation that rapidly clears away waste products and replaces blood with fresh nutrients.
- Massage relaxes tight muscles on an overworked cat. (An overworked cat?)
- Cat Massage is the fastest and surest way to produce a cat smile.

- Massaging your cat can alert you early to any unusual growths on or below the surface of the skin, and to any changes in your cat's health.
- You become more finely tuned to your cat's physical condition. You will have firsthand, up-to-date information about your cat, which will help during veterinary visits. An early diagnosis leads to a better prognosis.
- Cat Massage allows your cat to be accustomed to being handled. This is especially important to help make veterinary visits less frightening, or to allow for easier judging at cat shows.
- Your cat may allow you to clip the tips of her nails without complaint or fuss.
- Touch is powerful—it conveys love, deepens trust, and forges a friendship.
- For ailing and postoperative cats, Cat Massage can provide the perfect remedy. Be sure to ask your veterinarian for approval.
- You are certain to develop a stronger bond with your cat through regular Cat Massage sessions.

Soon you and your cat will discover your own particular reasons for Cat Massage. Write them here.

_____

_____

_____

_____

_____

WHY CAT MASSAGE?

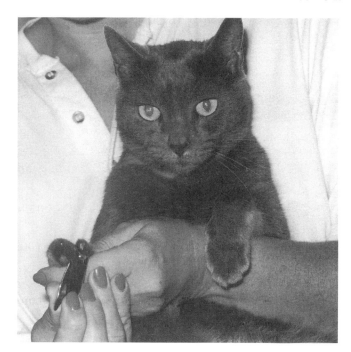

Massage makes mani-
cure time easier.

Cat Massage is sure to
produce a cat smile.

When to Cat Massage?

Cat Massage can be a few quick strokes on the way out to work, it can be five minutes of magical touch, or it can be a long, leisurely pampering session. That's for you and your cat to discover and decide together.

However rare, there may be times when your cat is not interested in Cat Massage. They may be few and far between, but kindly respect those boundaries. Every cat, even Champion, has moments of disinterest, and it's important to allow him that choice.

More often than not, Champion determines Cat Massage times. He will walk across my workspace and settle in my lap, unconcerned that I am intently working. *He* has decided that it's time for attention and affection. A few strokes for the keyboard, a few strokes for the cat.

In the beginning, you may find yourself initiating Cat Massage sessions. But I assure you, soon your cat will want more massaging. Then it's only a matter of time before your cat *demands* more massaging. Consider it a sign of progress and congratulate yourself.

Where to Cat Massage?

When it comes to where to Cat Massage, almost anything goes, so be creative.

- Mr. Tom or Miss Kitty sitting on your lap—the classic petting position, a tried-and-true winning spot.
- Cat being held in your arms—another good place to begin—what I call a frequent-feeler position. Even though this is a familiar position, be careful of any unexpected moves or loud noises. Your cat could react in haste and you could become a launching pad. Ouch!
- On a windowsill, ledge, or his preferred perch—a gesture of true accommodation on your part. Pull up a chair and caress kitty. You'll get a view of the world through feline eyes.
- At his favorite nook or cranny—follow your cat to his favorite resting place. This might mean under the kitchen table or at the top of the second-floor landing. If your cat likes the place, there must be a reason for it. The old saying "If the mountain won't go to Mohammed, Mohammed will go to the mountain" works for Cat Massage, too. Lately, my cat Champion is favoring the corner of the rug underneath my desk. A bit of a crawl for me, but, hey, that's called going the extra mile for love.
- On the floor—a great position, because here you are on

equal levels. Since humans stand taller than cats, most often they are looking up to us. In this position, however, there's eye-to-eye contact—a nose-to-whisker proximity that cats really enjoy. Lying down also gives your cat the opportunity to walk around the entire length of your body and explore you from a new perspective as well.

- Computer keyboards—an unusual and unexpected place, but once you've gotten the knack of Cat Massage, your cat will start visiting your work area (sprawl across it, actually) and purr requests for massage.

- On the couch—another horizontal position that affords great petting opportunities. Do you and your cat cozy up on the couch together? If so, that's great, because this new angle brings a new slant to massage. Stroking here encourages your cat to really extend his body with full stretches.

- Television watching—your cat's cue to be massaged, and commercials become so much more bearable with a cat curled up alongside you.

- On the bed—since bedtime is generally a tranquil time. Some of my best Cat Massage techniques were developed and practiced while in this comfortable environment. Champion got into the habit of resting alongside me while I prepared for sleep. He also rests *on* me, sprawling across my stomach, or sitting on my chest, so we're face-to-face. This position encourages great two-handed work. Bedtime became synonymous with massage time. A long, lazy, luxurious massage mellows us out. Falling asleep to the sound of contented purring is a joy. Upon awakening, morning massage starts our day. A frisky, more playful approach helps both of us wake up in a good mood.

- Cat sitting on a chair, couch, or bed, with you sitting below him—for all the reasons I just mentioned. This position guarantees that your cat will be at or above your eye level. He'll love you for this extra consideration, and a mega-meow moment might just occur.

WHERE TO MASSAGE? WHEREVER CAT IS:

In a bookcase,

even in a traveling box.

WHERE? ANYWHERE AND EVERYWHERE:

On the bed.

WHERE?

In the bag!

How Your Cat Works: Anatomy and Physiology Made Simple

There are only two basic components of Cat Massage. One is the masseuse or masseur—you. The other is the massagee—your cat. Your part is to supply the massaging instruments—your hands and fingers, the movements and the motions. Your feline friend simply provides the anatomy: the bones and muscles and functioning organs—all very live, beautifully organized material fashioned into one neat, compact animal. Let's take a look at your cat.

Your cat, of course, is a mammal of the family *Felidae*, a lithe-bodied, warm-blooded animal, obviously related to lions, tigers, cheetahs, panthers, and other glamorous wild creatures. Your cat's anatomy is certainly shaped and packaged quite differently from our own, but with all the component parts amazingly like ours. Their bones closely correspond to ours; their nervous system, muscles, circulation, and internal organs all function the same way our own working parts function.

If you know where your neck bones are, your shoulder blades, or your arm muscles, you can easily locate their counterparts on your cat. What is especially nice about Cat Massage is that this similarity in anatomy means that in most instances where massage feels good for you, it also feels good for your cat.

Feline Anatomy: What's Where

With only a few exceptions, we'll use human terms when referring to your cat's anatomy. We will refer to front and hindlegs rather than arms and legs; we will talk about paws and claws, not hands and fingernails. But as for nose, mouth, eyes, forehead, chin, throat, neck, shoulders, back, chest, and belly—your cat has them all, exactly where you'd expect them to be.

Quick Comparisons

	HUMANS	CATS
Anatomy	*Homo sapiens*	*Felis catus*
total bones	206	230
skull bones	22	35–40
total vertebral bones	26	49–53
neck bones	7	7 (even the tallest giraffes have 7)
pairs of ribs	12	13
adult teeth	32	30
gestation period	9 months	9 weeks (with 2–5 young per litter)
method of locomotion	biped (walking on 2 limbs)	quadruped (walking on 4 limbs)*
walking position	plantigrade (on the entire sole of the foot)	digitigrade (on the digits of the foot, with the remainder of the foot elevated)†

*This enables Cat to distribute his weight more evenly and achieve better balance.
†The cat has five digits (fingers) on each front leg, but only four on each back leg.

The Working Cat and How He Works

Let's look a little more closely at what goes on inside the sleek, supple body of a cat. You'll be better at Cat Massage if you can visualize what's there under the fur and how it works.

THE BONES: Your cat has 230 bones that, in a marvel of nature, form the skeletal framework around which the entire animal is constructed. Bones form the support for the standing cat, for the moving cat, and for the inner organs that maintain the living cat. Bones protect delicate structures: the skull for the brain, the rib cage for the heart and lungs, and the pelvis for the lower digestive system and the organs of reproduction. The skeleton, with its balanced system of joints, ligaments, and tendons allow the muscles to flex the limbs and move the cat. Together they enable your cat to creep, run, walk, climb, leap, curl up, roll over, whip its tail, and tear the stuffing out of a favorite toy.

THE MUSCLES: Essentially, since massage is for muscles, you'll need at least a nodding acquaintance with the major muscle groups. These are the voluntary muscles, the ones that respond when we consciously tell them what to do. They are coordinated; they know exactly what to do. When you turn a page in this book, voluntary muscles in your arm, hand, and fingers respond to your unspoken instruction. Muscles do many things. Most obvious, of course, is that they give your cat mobility— everything from mouse chasing to paw cleaning. Muscles also enable the body to maintain posture; without them, your cat could not stand, sit, or do much of anything.

A single muscle acting by itself rarely accomplishes a complex action. Most muscles work in groups. One muscle group will coordinate to flex a limb, and its corresponding muscle group will coordinate to extend it again. Therefore, in Cat Massage, you'll work on major muscle groups in a combination of massage strokes. Whenever possible, take a moment and explore your own muscles as you locate and massage the corresponding muscles that move your cat.

Some Major Muscles and Where They Function

There are literally dozens of muscles, big and small, near the surface and deep, involved in all cat movement. Some you may recognize from our corresponding human muscles. There are too many muscles to list, and certainly too many complicated Latin names to memorize. Since there's even too many to illustrate, the following list represents the muscles you'll become familiar with through Cat Massage.

> **Face and head:** For yawning, biting, chewing, swallowing, licking, and smiling. *Buccinator, digastric, masseter, temporal.*
>
> **Neck:** For turning, twisting, craning, and rotating. *Clavotrapezius, levator scapulae, sternomastoid.*
>
> **Shoulder and upper forearm:** For walking, running, stretching, climbing, and leaping. *Biceps, brachialis, deltoid, pectoral, trapezius, triceps.*
>
> **Back:** For turning, raising, arching, and stretching. *Erector spinae, external oblique, gluteals, latissimus dorsi.*
>
> **Thigh (shank) and upper hindleg:** For walking, climbing, leaping, running, and stretching. *Biceps femoris, gastrocnemius, quadriceps femoris, sartorius, tensor fascia latae.*
>
> **Abdomen:** Since this area is not protected by bony structures like the ribs, abdominal muscles compress the abdominal wall and hold the abdominal organs in place. *External and internal obliques, rectus and transversus abdominis.*

Paw: For scratching, stretching, and washing the other paw.

Digitorum brevis: extensor and flexor.

Tail: For flicking and swishing. *Has no muscles of its own:* the tail is controlled by the muscles of the lower back.

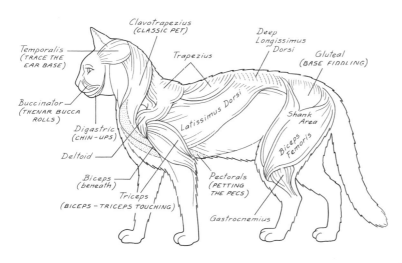

Muscular System

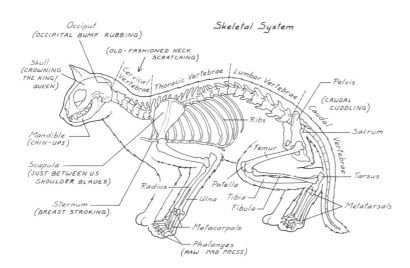

Skeletal System

Coming in for the Landing: How to Approach Your Cat for Cat Massage

The initial contact between Cat and hand is important because it sets the pace for the massage. Make it gentle, friendly, and inviting. If the approach to your cat consists of chasing her down the hallway, across the room, and cornering her on the floor, this will not set the mood for a successful massage.

Cats like a gradual approach. Remember, their belief system is centered in the knowledge that they, at all times, are running the show, so let's help them maintain their feline superiority.

Champion and I have been partners since 1983 and I still respect his right to a gentle approach from me. Here's how I do it—how Champ taught me: I always drop my hand, at a slight distance, to his eye level or lower. Then I slowly bring my hand in for Champion to sniff, recognize, and accept—both my scent and me. Allow for that necessary moment of awareness and agreement. This gives the cat a chance to get involved, too. Often Champion will signal his interest in a Cat Massage session in the same way—he'll approach me, sniff, and start rubbing his face and cheek against my hand or ankle. Or he'll simply give me a knowing look and a requesting meow. He'll signal his (rare) disinterest by simply walking away.

Before I ever pick Champion up, I always verbally alert him to my presence and intention. This is best accomplished with a soothing tone to my voice as I approach him—something like, "Hello my good-looking cat, how are you?" Any of our established phrases like "Handsome Champson" spoken in rhythmic familiarity establish initial contact.

Similarly, approach a new cat for the first time in the same way, just with more patience. Encourage Cat to become familiar with your voice, movements, and then hands. Allow Cat to rub against *your* hand. Let him initiate contact. When he's ready, touch him on his shoulder. This is much less intimidating for Cat than being touched on his face.

The Tools and Techniques of the Trade

Let's paws for a moment to become familiar with the instruments that will be doing Cat Massage—your hands. They are amazing structures, each with twenty muscles and twenty-seven bones. The Tools and Techniques of the Trade are Hand Parts, Hand Positions, Motion, Speed, Pressure, and Mood.

Hand Parts

You will use twelve different parts of your hand with Cat Massage. They are:

Finger pads	*Knuckle nooks*	*Open palm*	*Two fingers*
Fingertips	*Thumb*	*Closed palm*	*Finger sides*
Knuckles	*Thumb pad*	*Four fingers*	*Thenar Eminence*

Finger pads: These are the soft, cushiony parts of the fingers—they house your fingerprints.

Fingertips: The area located above the finger pads: some end at the top of your fingers, or if you have long nails, at the tip of your fingernails.

Knuckles: Bend your fingers and notice that there are two knuckles that form—*not* your fist knuckles. One row of knuckles is the angle (or bumps) closer to your fingernails, the other row of knuckles is closer to the base of your fingers. These are the knuckles to use.

Knuckle nooks: There are two. One is the short, flat surface closer to your fingernails. The other nook is the broader surface extending back toward your fist knuckles. Easy, isn't it?

Thumb: Either thumb, its tip and side.

Thumb pad: The soft, cushiony part of your thumb.

Open palm: Full hand, from fingertips to wrist, with fingers spread wide.

Closed palm: Same as open palm but with fingers together.

Four fingers: This is simply using four fingers together—index, middle, ring, and pinky. It can be palm up or palm down.

Two fingers: This is just like four fingers except using any two: index and middle together or ring and pinky together.

Finger sides: This is simply the sides of any or all of your four fingers: index, middle, ring, and pinky.

Thenar eminence: Technical name for a familiar hand part. Look at your hand, palm up. The fleshy part that extends below the thumb, almost midway to your palm is your thenar eminence. Thenar means relating to the palm, and eminence means height. See how simple this is?

1. Closed palm, four fingers
2. Two fingers
3. Knuckle nooks
4. Open palm

Take a moment now and locate these parts on your own hand.

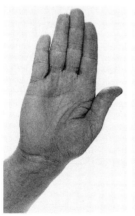

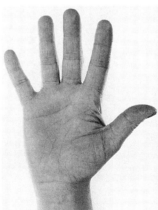

1   2   3   4

Hand Positions

There are six different ways to position your hand with Cat Massage. They are:

Palm up	*Horizontal*	*Cupping*
Palm down	*Vertical*	*Horseshoe*

Palm up: The palm portion faces up—this way, you see your fingerprints.

Palm down: The palm portion faces down—this way, you see your fingernails.

Horizontal: The palm faces sideways along the cat—this way, your fingertips are pointing up toward the spine.

Vertical: The palm faces lengthwise along the cat—this way, your fingertips are pointing toward the cat's head and your palm is parallel to the spine.

Cupping: Palm up, all fingers together—this curved position creates a resting place for your cat's head or chin.

Horseshoe: Four fingers together, curved, with thumb separate and also curved. The letter "C" is a horizontal horseshoe; an upside-down "U" is a vertical horseshoe.

Take a moment to explore these hand positions. Note that the Hand Position (in the actual massage techniques) refers to the *starting position*. If you're right-handed, use your right hand. Left-handers use your left. With time and practice, you can alternate. Most movements here are described for using one hand at a time. If and when you can coordinate the same technique on the other side of the cat and use both hands, good for you. Double your pleasure, double your fun.

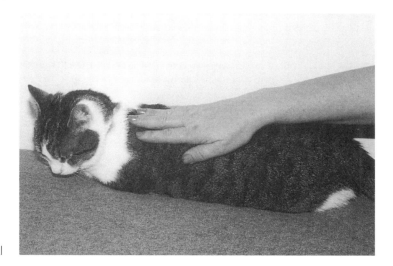

Vertical

Horizontal and cupping

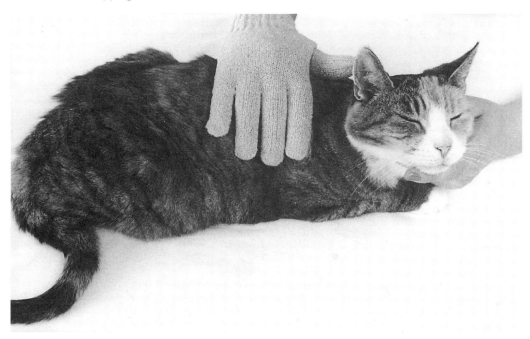

Vertical horseshoe

Motion

This refers to the action we create from our hand parts and positions—in which way and direction a technique works best. We don't want to be ruffling anyone's fur when we mean to give a graceful gliding motion.

There are six basic motions or strokes you'll use as building blocks for your Cat Massage techniques:

Gliding	*Circling*	*Kneading*
Waving	*Flicking*	*Rubbing*

It's more than just "going through the motions" to give our cat the best Cat Massage we can give. Take some time to practice these motions—perhaps on a pillow or a stuffed animal—and then on your cat.

Gliding: We're all familiar with those long, loving caresses that Cat loves so well. Gliding is the classic massage stroke, a straight, flowing, continuous motion. The direction is always toward the tail, down the length of the body. Take your hand off Cat at the end of the stroke, bring it back up, and glide it down again. The glide back up is called the return stroke. If you choose to keep your hand on Cat during the return stroke, make sure you lighten the pressure. Essentially, gliding is what you do when you pet your cat. This is the simplest of all massage strokes, and the one most frequently used. The corresponding human massage stroke for gliding is a French term called *effleurage*. There's an old saying I learned while in school: "When in doubt, *effleurage*." It works on people and it works on cats. You can never go wrong with gentle gliding. It always fits in. For gliding, you can use any part of your hand. Begin by learning with palm (open or closed), practice with fingertips and finger pads, and advance to using knuckles and knuckle nooks. The entire massage session can be done just with gliding—it's a great all-around, all-purpose stroke.

Waving: Compare the side-to-side rocking motion of your hand, with fingers kept flat, to the action of a windshield wiper, or waving good-bye. This is waving, a stroke that can be either horizontal or vertical, with fingers together or spread wide using the same pressure back and forth. With horizontal waving, your palm and fingers sweep alongside Cat's body, fingers pointing up toward the spine. With vertical waving, your hand sweeps the length of Cat, with your fingers along the spine. Waving works well on large, broad areas, like the back and sides. When you're more comfortable and practiced with this stroke, and you want a variation, try strumming. Strumming uses the same motion as waving, but with the tips of the fingers bent, like strumming a banjo. Finger-pad and fingertip strumming work well on smaller areas like the head and neck. Even knuckle nooks can be used for this stroke. Your cat will delightfully help you determine the details.

Circling: Just like the name suggests, this is creating circles. Make tiny circles, barely the size of a dime, with your fingertips. Or make slightly larger circles, half-dollar shaped, with your finger pads. Watch tender boundaries, like the ears and whiskers, and follow the contours of your cat. Fingers flat together make even larger circles on wider areas like shoulders, back, and sides. Circles can be clockwise or counterclockwise—your choice. As with the other motions, different hand parts can be used, depending on your experience and expertise.

Flicking: This involves the fingers rather than the entire hand. Imagine flicking many crumbs off a table, one by one. Or, imagine flicking to be the motion created by pressing down on a pump dispenser. Flick with either one, two, or three fingers, depending on the area. The thumb usually flicks alone. Light flicking barely makes contact with fur; slow, mild flicking allows you to feel the bony structures beneath the fur.

Kneading: Now, wait a moment here. I'm not talking about the kind of manipulating a baker performs when preparing loaves of bread. My kneading is a gentle caress, a squeezing, almost "milking" motion. It uses the flicking motion with all five fingers and palm—in the horseshoe position. Add a slight dip down when all fingers are extended, and a slight pull up when the fingers are brought together. This works great along the entire spine, and is a more advanced stroke, so take your time before trying this one.

Rubbing: This is pretty self-explanatory. You'll move along Cat's body exerting pressure as indicated in the Pressure Technique.

Cat Massage is neither planned, choreographed, nor perfectly coordinated. Some of the best responses you'll generate will come from gently going with the flow, following sequences as they come up, or creating new motions of your own. Once you understand the basics, you're free to enjoy and explore all the delights of Cat Massage. Take a moment to practice these strokes. Now that hand parts, hand positions, and the appropriate stroking motions have been addressed, it's time to add a few more ingredients into our banquet of Cat Massage delights—speed, pressure, and mood.

Speed

Life today is rush, rush, rush. Everybody's in a (legitimate) hurry all the time, and too often we maintain a pace just shy of frenzy. Right? Please understand that it doesn't work that way in Cat Massage. One purpose for Cat Massage is to create soothing, peaceful times with your cat, and that starts with the speed of your work. Remember, Cat Massage has no rushed pace, only re-laxing rhythms. Good Cat Massage can be hypnotic, lulling—almost mesmerizing. There are four speeds for Cat Massage:

Slow-mo   *No-mo*   *Leisurely*   *Fast 'n frisky*

Slow-mo (*slow motion*): "Easy does it" is a good way to live life, and a great way to do Cat Massage. This is the pre-ferred pace for most purposeful petting, because it works, especially in detailed areas like the head, neck, and shoul-ders. What may seem like an excruciatingly slow stroke to you can feel so appropriate to your feline who is receiving the touch. When they are not chasing butterflies, running across lawns, or racing to the food bowl, cats tend to be low-activity animals. Most prefer a mellow touch.

No-mo (*no motion*): This is even slower than slow-mo, and it's just what the name implies—no motion at all. It's sim-ply letting your palm, finger, or fingers rest comfortably on your cat. That's it—no movement, no action necessary. Feel the bonding that comes from just being together. Feel the rhythmic motion of your cat's breathing, follow the rise and fall of her respiration, and let Cat feel the warmth of your hands. For an interesting variation, try this: Instead of resting your hand on Cat, allow Cat to rest on you—sup-port your cupped hand under her chin so she can rest her head on your palm. Or let her position her front paws on top of your arm, just for a change of pace. Being still, being peaceful is comfortable and familiar to cats, and the idea of a no-mo stroke just might be appealing. Try it.

Leisurely: This is comfortable caressing, gently weaving in and around your cat's contours. Think of it as an enjoyable, relaxed pace, faster than slow-mo or no-mo, but still far from fast 'n frisky.

Fast 'n frisky: This is probably the speed that is initially most appealing until you see and feel the pleasure in slower stroking. Certain techniques and times do specify your touch to be fast 'n frisky, like the ruffling motion used in

Base Fiddling (see p. 63). Vigorous massage strokes incorporate quicker movements on broader areas, like the back.

Pressure

Like slower speeds, lighter pressure works better. In gliding strokes, for example, the flowing motion is directed toward the tail, and so is the pressure. This one-way pressure increases circulation in that area. Instead of releasing your hand, keep it on Cat as you bring your hand back up (on the return stroke). Just make sure the pressure is considerably lighter. This lighter pressure is necessary because sustained pressure back and forth creates confusion with the muscles and blood circulation we affect with Cat Massage. Exceptions are with the waving (strumming) strokes, which purposely ruffle small areas for short times to increase blood flow and relax tight muscles. Our four pressure choices include:

Featherlight   *Light*   *Mild*   *Deep*

Featherlight: This is an airy touch, barely making contact with the cat. Just feel for fur. Work this featherlightly and you'll generate interesting responses. Featherlight pressure is ethereal, like the touch of a fairy.

Light: This is comfortable caressing, tender touching, and subtle stroking. With light pressure we feel fur and anatomical landmarks below, bones like the occiput (bump at the back of Cat's head) or broad areas like the belly. Light pressure is calm, soothing, and gentle.

Mild: This is working a bit deeper. You'll use this pressure more often, once you're comfortable with your cat's preferences. It's locating and feeling the bony landmarks under the fur. With practice, mild pressure allows you to feel the ridges of the triangular-shaped scapula, explore the bumpy protuberances along the spine, or examine the smooth contours of your cat's head. Combine light and mild pressures for the best Cat Massage results.

Deep: This is more exploratory, more probing, and also more careful work. Deep work may be allowed in the shoulder area—between the scapula and the spine. Deep pressure is best used with a gentling gliding stroke, usually along the length of the spine. Always remember to use lighter pressure with the return stroke. Deeper work demands focused attention, patience, and awareness. It is a *slower* Cat Massage. If your cat's feedback encourages deep work, do so, with practice. Otherwise, get creative with featherlight, light, and mild pressures.

Mood

Always keep in mind the mood created by your environment. Is it a good time for Cat Massage? Keep your environment calm and your background in synch with a massage. A house full of frenetic activity puts neither of you at ease. Reserve Cat Massage for special times, and set the pace for a winning session. There are three moods to match the speed and pressure of Cat Massage:

Gentle and relaxed   *Playful*   *Frolicky fun*

Gentle and relaxed: This is what you would expect from long, languid stroking. It's soothing, loving, and full of ease. The mood is as gentle and relaxed for you as it is for your cat.

Playful: This is similar to a leisurely pace in speed. A playful mood is lighthearted. Both massager and massagee are enjoying themselves, having fun, and it shows.

Frolicky fun: This is animated, amusing, and enthusiastic.

Feline Feedback: Friendly and Unfriendly Responses

How to Know if You Are Giving a Good Cat Massage

Relax—you have the best teacher available, Cat. She will provide the obvious and subtle signals of advice and adjustment—feline feedback. Look carefully, listen, and take suggestions. By learning to read your cat's reactions, you'll develop a new insight—a better understanding of what she wants and doesn't want. You will be thrilled when you get a hearty "two paws up!"

Signals of Friendly Feedback

Cat sticking around: This is the most obvious and easy to see. There is only one reason why a cat does anything, and that's because a cat wants to.

Purring: This is another immediate result that lets you know you are doing the right thing. From a sewing machine hum to a Harley Davidson roar, this says that your touch (and you) are appreciated. When the purring becomes excessive, I call it power purring.

Kneading: This display of affection tells you that when Cat kneads you, she really needs you! Opening and closing the paws in rhythmic action returns a cat back to kittenhood days, when suckling on her mother was both a joy and a necessity. Air kneading is a good activity for a cat to flex her many paw muscles. Special kneading techniques are included in the Paws and Claws chapter (see pp. 107–111).

Eyes blinking dreamily: Soft opening and closing of eyes conveys soothing approval.

Body stretching: This is when Cat moves up and manipulates himself to accommodate and/or anticipate your massage. Around the neck area, Champion will crane his neck to guide me along and maneuver my stroke to his precise desires. Spackle Cat will push herself forward for further petting. And on the flip side, Francesca Cat will simply flop on her side. Recognize these moves? Body stretching includes that triumphant time when your cat rolls over onto his back and exposes his belly in a vulnerable position for him and a tribute to you.

Cat smiling: We've all seen cat smiles and they're glorious. Need I say more?

Cat kissing: These little licks and sniffs are nontraditional kisses as we know them, but feline for sure.

Response rubbing: This is when Cat returns your caresses with caresses of her own, her face rubbing back against your hand, her body brushing along your leg, curling around your ankle, or the sandpapery feel of her tongue licking you.

Tail flicking: From an occasional flick to a steady rhythm, tail flicking is another way Cat participates in his massage session.

Drooling: KitKat showed me this one. In her case, a drooler is not a person specializing in rings and watches, it's a cat who's so wrapped up in enjoying a massage that she forgets to swallow—then she drools. Silly as it may sound, this is a very expressive and an unconscious form of approval. Remember, you can't fool drool.

Meowing: Do you have a talker? A talker is a cat who expresses himself clearly and verbally. Not to be confused with purring. General conversation includes the short, "mrw" to the full "Meeeooowww."

Playful nipping: Sometimes Champion will gently bite the back of my hand—it's his way of responding with the closest things available, his teeth. No cause for alarm, though, unless Cat happens to be a real tiger.

Cat demanding massage: This is when Cat shows up and will not leave without some massaging. When a full food bowl won't appease her, assorted cat toys won't sway her interest, and all the birds in town can't coax her away, no matter how busy you might be—massage she wants, and massage she'll get.

Rubbing: When Cat picks up the pace and continues to rub up against me, I call that Cat Massage Me.

Sleeping: This shows that your pet trusts you enough to let down her cat guard, and she relaxes deeply because of your loving touch. What a marvelous display of complacent contentment—a sleeping cat.

Other friendly feedback from my feline:

_____

_____

_____

_____

_____

Signals of Unfriendly Feedback

There are two sides to every coin and every Cat Massage. Unfriendly feedback is no cause for consternation or insecurity, because it's helpful. Not criticism, it simply asks that you adjust your style. Think of it this way: Cat is offering a qualified opinion to improve your technique. Be prepared for these warning signals—in fact, look for them, because the more you can find, the more you can fix. And the more you fix, the better you will Cat Massage.

There's less on this list, because most cats like massage most of the time. With time and with practice, this list will grow even shorter as your friendly-feedback signals grow longer. Listen and follow suggestions. Remember that adaptability and the willingness to change are key components for Cat Massage success. Go with the flow—what may be a favorite this week can drop to low stroke on the totem pole next week. Make it easy for your cat to share unfriendly feedback with you. It's the best way to learn.

Cat moving away: This shows obvious disinterest. Don't take it personally—Cat may simply not be in the mood.

Unplayful nipping: Instead of the gentle biting seen in playful nipping, take this biting remark to say "No thanks, not now." Heed the message.

Scratching: If your cat scratches you, scratch what you're doing.

Hissing: If Cat's ears are flattened back in a guarded position—a cat scowl—and he begins to hiss, take a cue and take a hike.

Back sinking low: Upon touching, if your cat's back sinks low to the ground, she's obviously not impressed.

Any unusual, negative, or out-of-character behavior: This means cool it for now.

Just remember, there can always be times when, for whatever reason, a Cat Massage won't work. No big deal.

How my cat says "Thanks, but no thanks."

_____

_____

_____

Some unfriendly feedback is short-term while Cat becomes accustomed to a certain stroke, and other feedback is long-term. Francesca will tolerate no tummy touching, yet Groundhog goes belly up as soon as someone is near him. Go figure. So, if you find one technique isn't quite your cat's meow, simply move onto another. There's plenty of your cat to massage, and plenty of massage for your cat.

Let's Try Cat Massage!

At this point, you're probably eager to try your hand at Cat Massage. If that's the case, go ahead! Give it a try! Keep in mind all the information you've just read, and refer back to it as often as you need to make sure you're on the right track. With the guiding help of your cat, you'll do just fine!

GETTING INTO IT HEAD FIRST

Crowning the King/Queen: A Royal Touch
Trace the Ear Base
The Graceful Gliding Swoop
Chin-Ups: My Purr-sonal Favorite
Chinny Chin Chin
Apex Flicking
Francesca's Forehead Favorite
Thenar *Bucca* Rolls
Check Out Those Cheeks: A Facial Favorite
Side of the Head Stroking: Champion's Favorite
Fingertips and Whisker Beds
Head Horseshoes

The head is an ideal place to begin Cat Massage, so let's take it from the top. Your cat has probably already told you this by stretching his head to meet your extended hand. The head is a particularly sensitive area, especially the face, so be careful here. All the organs of sense and orientation are located here: the eyes, nose, mouth, whiskers, and ears. Keep massage motions slow and consistent in pressure and speed. Listen and watch closely: Your cat will move his head to maximize his pleasure, and will tell you instantly if he is displeased or uncomfortable. And watch your fingernails: If they are sharp, be careful to avoid damage to eyes, ears, or nose.

HEAD TIPS: Since the head area is small and sensitive, massage strokes here will be circling, flicking, and gentle rubbing or waving, with no kneading.

A SPECIAL PRECAUTION: If more than one speed, pressure, or mood is listed in each of the Cat Massage techniques that follow, always begin with the first one. If Cat allows, then build up to a faster pace, a different pressure, or a livelier mood. Always remember that your cat is the boss. If she does not like a particular technique, please do not force her to participate. With time and patience, she'll come to love these massage sessions.

Crowning the King/Queen: A Royal Touch

AREA: Top of the head—from forehead to back of neck; side to side—from ear to ear.

HAND PARTS: Finger pads, fingertips, thumb pad, knuckles, knuckle nooks.

HAND POSITION: Palm down.

MOTION: Circling.

SPEED: Slow-mo, leisurely.

PRESSURE: Featherlight, light, mild.

MOOD: Gentle and relaxed, playful.

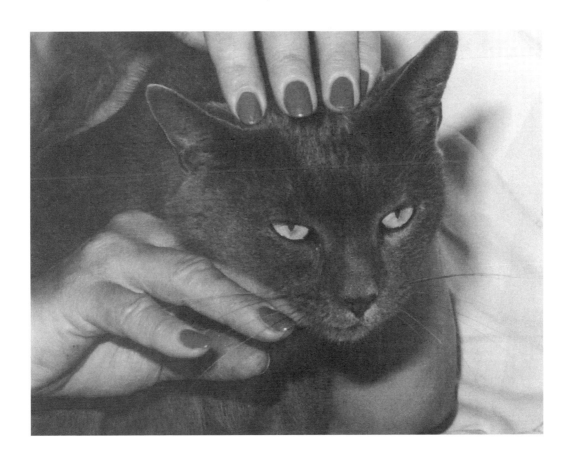

TECHNIQUE: With finger pads and fingertips, pattern clockwise or counterclockwise circles on top of Cat's head. Make small circles and cover the boundaries of the forehead, neck, and ears. Then make tiny circles with your finger pads barely moving at all. Alternate these with larger circles, wide enough to cover the entire top of his head. Vary your pressure. The featherlight movements will barely make surface contact with fur. The light and mild pressures allow you to feel the bony parts of the head and neck. Soon Cat will be moving his head in response to your fingers. Now try this move with your thumb pad.

CAUTION: Since this is your first Cat Massage technique, start off slowly and easily.

My Cat
Likes   _____

My Cat
Really Likes _____

ADVANCED TECHNIQUE: Use knuckles or knuckle nooks. This is a good lead-in to *Trace the Ear Base*.

Trace the Ear Base

AREA: Base of Cat's ear.
HAND PARTS: Finger pads, two fingers, thumb.
HAND POSITION: Horizontal.
MOTION: Circling, rubbing.
SPEED: Slow-mo, leisurely.
PRESSURE: Featherlight, light.
MOOD: Gentle and relaxed.

TECHNIQUE: Slowly trace tiny clockwise circles with your finger pads below the base of Cat's ear. This is the area directly below the ear opening—*not* the opening itself. Perhaps Cat will twist and rotate his head against your head in playful delight.

CAUTION: There's heightened sensitivity here because of the ear, so keep the mood gentle and relaxed.

ADVANCED TECHNIQUE: Some cats (not Champion) encourage light massaging of the ear itself. Slowly caress the ear with the index and middle fingers together, the ear in the middle, and the thumb below. Rub carefully and slowly.

My Cat
Likes   _____

My Cat
Really Likes   _____

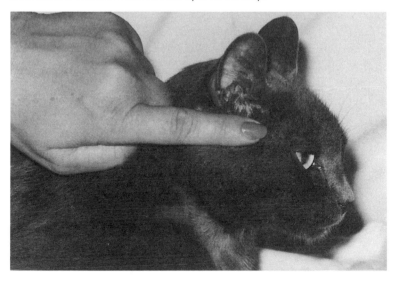

The Graceful Gliding Swoop

AREA: Top and sides of the head, under the chin.
HAND PARTS: Finger pads, four fingers.
HAND POSITION: Cupping.
MOTION: Gliding.
SPEED: Slow-mo, leisurely.
PRESSURE: Light.
MOOD: Gentle and relaxed.

TECHNIQUE: Begin with finger pads on the forehead. Follow the contour of the head. Go down behind the ears along the cheek and under the chin. Continue to glide right on out to the tip of the chin and off. This movement is like a wide letter "C" scoop. Practicing will enable the movement to become a graceful gliding swoop.

CAUTION: Keep pressure light, especially around the throat.

My Cat
Likes   _____

My Cat
Really Likes   _____

VARIATION: Use four fingers and reverse direction. Start from the chin and follow up to the ear. Follow this technique with *Chin-Ups* and *Chinny Chin Chin*.

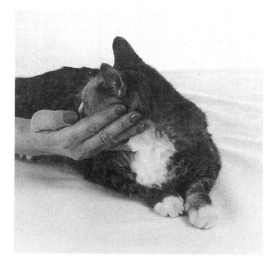
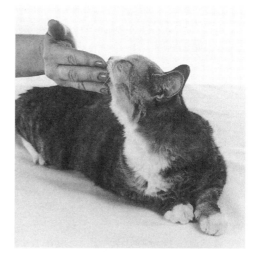

Chin-ups: My Purr-sonal Favorite

AREA: The entire triangular chin area, from the back of the throat to the tip of the chin.

HAND PARTS: Finger pads, fingertips, finger sides, two fingers, four fingers, closed palm, thumb.

HAND POSITION: Palm up, cupping.

MOTION: Circling, rubbing.

SPEED: Slow-mo, no-mo.

PRESSURE: Featherlight, light.

MOOD: Gentle and relaxed.

TECHNIQUE: Use your finger pads to stroke under the chin in a circular motion. When you're comfortable in that small area, and with Cat's approval, you can alternate with fingertips and finger sides, and lightly rub back and forth, from the throat to the tip of the chin. The clearest indication of technique approval is for your cat to crane his head up, chin pointing toward the sky. This is pure, positive feline feedback, and seems to happen automatically. When it does, you'll know you're right on target. Now you can even continue this light rubbing on the front of his neck. *Be careful* of the windpipe here!

ADVANCED TECHNIQUE: Using two or four fingers or closed palm, cup Cat's head in your hand, and let it rest there, not moving at all. This is surprisingly relaxing, and a technique where no-mo can be most effective. Continue cupping Cat's head in your palm, and see if you can coordinate gently moving your thumb in circles under his chin.

My Cat
Likes   _____

My Cat
Really Likes _____

Chinny Chin Chin

AREA: Tip of chin.
HAND PARTS: Finger pads, fingertips.
HAND POSITION: Palm up.
MOTION: Circling, rubbing.
SPEED: Slow-mo, no-mo.
PRESSURE: Featherlight, light.
MOOD: Gentle and relaxed.

TECHNIQUE: After a few circular *Chin-Ups*, instead of continuing off the chin, stay at the tip of the chin and rub Mr. Tom's beard back and forth or perhaps Miss Kitty's soft facial fur. Keep your fingers still (in no-mo) and allow your feline friend to rub against you.

My Cat Likes _____

My Cat Really Likes _____

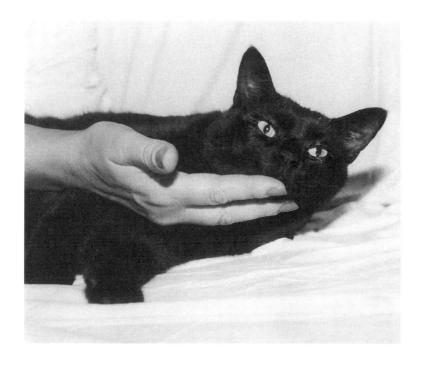

Apex Flicking

AREA: The top of the head—from the highest point to the neck.
HAND PART: Fingertips.
HAND POSITION: Palm down.
MOTION: Flicking.
SPEED: Slow-mo, leisurely.
PRESSURE: Featherlight, light.
MOOD: Playful.

TECHNIQUE: Begin gentle fingertip flicking across the top of the head with either the index finger, middle finger, or both. Follow over to the base of each ear and back to center, and cover part of the neck.

My Cat
Likes   _____

My Cat
Really Likes   _____

CAUTION: This stroke is well suited for longer fingernails, but be careful not to scratch, especially around the ears.

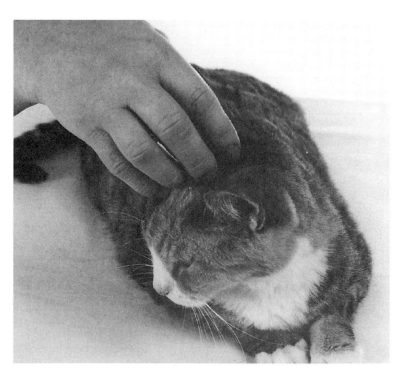

Francesca's Forehead Favorite

AREA: Forehead—the inverted triangle between the ears down
   to the tip of the nose.
HAND PARTS: Two fingers, four fingers, finger pads, fingertips.
HAND POSITION: Horizontal.
MOTION: Rubbing.
SPEED: Slow-mo, leisurely.
PRESSURE: Featherlight, light, mild.
MOOD: Gentle and relaxed.

TECHNIQUE: With two or four fingers (or even one or three) in
a horizontal position, rub your finger pads and fingertips up and
down Cat's forehead—*not* across in a sawing motion. Cover all
areas on the top of your cat's head—she'll show you where to
massage.

VARIATION: When using four fingers, lift one or two fingers,
stroke back and forth a few times, replace them, and lift different fingers.

My Cat
Likes   _____
My Cat
Really Likes   _____

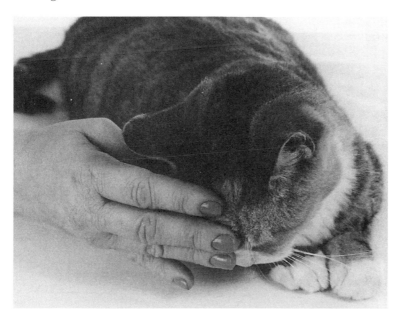

Thenar Bucca Rolls

AREA: Cat cheeks (*buccae*), behind the whiskers, closer to the back of the head.
HAND PARTS: Thumbs, thenar eminences, open palms.
HAND POSITIONS: Palms up, cupping.
MOTION: Rubbing, circling.
SPEED: No-mo, slow-mo.
PRESSURE: Light.
MOOD: Gentle and relaxed.

TECHNIQUE: This is a fancy name for the coordinated rubbing of your thumbs and thenar eminences (the fleshy part of the palms below the thumbs), against your cat's cheeks. It's a bit tricky to learn, but truly welcomed. When Cat is resting on your chest, face-to-face, put your open palms under his head, a few inches apart. With his head resting in your palms, you can enjoy a no-mo moment. Then make slow circles around his cheek area, *clockwise only* (counterclockwise is too ruffling for such a tender area), and let him rub back in response to you.

CAUTION: A whisker watch is in alert here. Stay behind them, closer to the ears, and be careful not to bend them backward. Note: This technique is not for all cats.

ADVANCED TECHNIQUE: Rub circles in unison, then alternate the pattern, so that while the right palm is at the top of the circle on one side of the cheek, the left palm is at the bottom of the circle on the side of the other cheek.

My Cat
Likes   _____

My Cat
Really Likes   _____

Check Out Those Cheeks: A Facial Favorite

AREA: Cheek, in front of the ear line—right around the whisker beds.

HAND PARTS: Thumb pad, finger pads, fingertips, finger sides, knuckles, knuckle nooks.

HAND POSITION: Cupping.

MOTION: Circling, rubbing.

SPEED: Slow-mo.

PRESSURE: Light, mild, featherlight.

MOOD: Gentle and relaxed, playful.

TECHNIQUE: Caress the cheeks slowly and carefully. With thumb pad, finger pads, fingertips, and finger sides, massage tenderly using small circles and short rubs. Use light and mild pressures. Then for an interesting change of pace, work featherlight. Because this area is so sensitive, Cat will respond with pleasure to the changes in pressure. He may even begin to rub his head against your fingers in appreciation. Add some knuckles and knuckle nooks now.

My Cat
Likes   _____

My Cat
Really Likes   _____

CAUTION: A whisker watch alert is in effect here. Remember that whiskers are sensitive—so be careful to not bend them backward or forward.

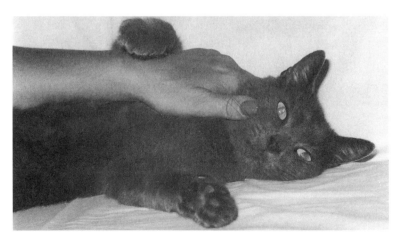

Side of the Head Stroking: Champion's Favorite

AREA: Side of the head, behind and under the ear line.
HAND PARTS: Knuckles, knuckle nooks, four fingers, finger pads, fingertips.
HAND POSITION: Vertical.
MOTION: Waving, circling.
SPEED: Slow-mo, leisurely, fast 'n frisky.
PRESSURE: Light, mild, deep.
MOOD: Gentle and relaxed, playful, frolicky fun.

TECHNIQUE: After you *Check Out Those Cheeks,* caress the side part of Cat's face. With this technique, you caress using all of the hand parts listed. Wave up and down, side to side, and all around this area in a strumming motion. You may also create circles. This is a major response area. Enjoy the feedback.

My Cat Likes _____

My Cat Really Likes _____

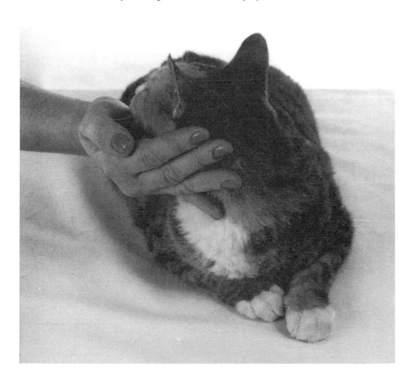

Fingertips and Whisker Beds

AREA: Area around the base of the whiskers.
HAND PARTS: Finger pads, fingertips.
HAND POSITION: Vertical.
MOTION: Circling.
SPEED: Slow-mo.
PRESSURE: Featherlight.
MOOD: Gentle and relaxed.

TECHNIQUE: Massage the head for a few minutes so that the area—and the cat—are warmed up. *Ever so slowly and with the barest pressure,* trace tiny circles along the whisker beds—the base of the whiskers where they attach to your cat's cheek. *Do not* massage the actual whiskers.

CAUTION: A major whisker watch alert is in effect here. No touching and no bending them. Please be very patient and very careful here because everything is so sensitive. Heightened sensitivity makes an area feel so very good when done so very lightly.

My Cat
Likes   _____

My Cat
Really Likes   _____

Head Horseshoes

AREA: Cat's head—near the ear.
HAND PARTS: Finger pads, fingertips, four fingers.
HAND POSITIONS: Horizontal, horseshoe.
MOTION: Waving.
SPEED: Slow-mo.
PRESSURE: Light.
MOOD: Gentle and relaxed.

TECHNIQUE: If Cat permits, fit his head in your horseshoe-shaped hand. Your fingers will cover the top of Cat's head, your thumb will cover the chin. Cat's head will be in the middle. Let the fit be enough to support the weight of the head, and loose enough to be comfortable. Slowly wave back and forth from the tip of his chin and nose on top. Also go from the forehead to the throat.

ADVANCED TECHNIQUE: Pull your horseshoe out a bit from the head, and reposition behind the ear. Continue rhythmic waving.

My Cat
Likes   ____

My Cat
Really Likes   ____

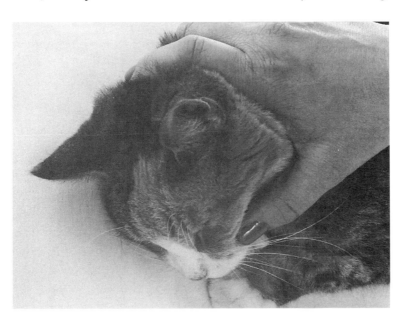

BACK FOR MORE

The Grand *Effleurage*: The Master Stroke of Cat Massage
Hand Over Hand and Down We Go: A Two-handed Double
    Delight
Base Fiddling: Rump Ruffling
Ruffling Shuffle
Back Horseshoes
Spine Tingling
Alternate Circular Side Waving
Farewell Flourishes

The back is a great area to massage! It is big, it is uncomplicated, it offers endless possibilities. It is often the starting point, with *The Grand Effleurage*, and can also serve to end a massage session with *Farewell Flourishes*. The back is the alpha and the omega of Cat Massage. Many back strokes are among the easiest to learn. They provide good practice to build courage and confidence so you'll want to continue onto more detailed and involved work.

The back, like the head, is ideal territory for establishing contact and introducing your hands to your cat's body. Some cats flinch at first contact with the lower-back area, so approach this area cautiously. Back for More and Side Stroking techniques often work hand in hand. Learning good back work is essential for happy massage sessions; expert technique here will keep your cat coming back for more.

BACK NOTES: Notice that there are many variations in each of the following techniques—opportunities for the full range of hand parts, hand positions, motions, speeds, pressures, and moods. Strokes here are wider, and with more area to cover, we see more gliding, strumming, and ruffling. Wearing gloves gives a different texture. Try it. Speeds can get faster, pressures deeper, and the mood swings are welcomed here, from gentle and relaxed to playful and frolicky fun. Enjoy! Notice also that an individual technique can be so detailed that it's the only technique used for an entire session. Read on—you'll see what I mean.

The Grand Effleurage: The Master Stroke of Cat Massage

AREA: The entire length of the back and the broad sides of the cat.

HAND PARTS: Palm (open or closed), finger pads, fingertips.

HAND POSITION: Palm down.

MOTION: Gliding.

SPEED: Slow-mo, leisurely, fast 'n frisky.

PRESSURE: Featherlight, light, mild, deep.

MOOD: Gentle and relaxed, playful, frolicky fun.

TECHNIQUE: Start high up behind the ears. With palm open or closed, run your hand all the way down the length of Cat's back. Continue down to the end of her back, right to the tip of her tail. If, of course, Cat is a Manx, then continue to the end of her back (to her dimple if she's a rumpy Manx; to her tail stump if she's a stumpy Manx). Follow this for any of the techniques that

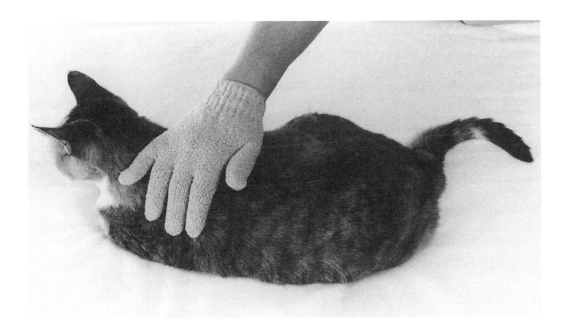

instruct you to massage to the tip of the tail. Don't stop at mid or low back. It's like half a handshake. Repeat a few times for familiarity. Now get very creative and playful with this technique. Change from using your palm to using your finger pads. Run them along her sleek back, and then bend your fingers and allow the fingertips to slide along. Cover the top of her back, down both sides of her spine, then use long, gliding strokes along her sides.

This technique allows for the most flexibility of all strokes, so take advantage of it. Vary your pressure and speed. Explore the range of options. Start with featherlight pressure, and gradually increase to as deep as she allows. Vary from slow-mo right up to fast 'n frisky, with her assent. Discover the true beauty of this technique. You'll see and feel how *The Grand Effleurage* can be gentle and relaxed, playful, and frolicky fun. An entire massage session can be built around this one major technique, which you'll understand when you're finished with it.

My Cat
Likes   _____

My Cat
Really Likes   _____

Hand Over Hand and Down We Go: A Two-handed Double Delight

AREA: Back.
HAND PARTS: Palms (open and closed).
HAND POSITIONS: Horizontal, vertical.
MOTION: Gliding.
SPEED: Slow-mo, leisurely, fast 'n frisky.
PRESSURE: Light, mild, deep.
MOOD: Gentle and relaxed, playful.

TECHNIQUE: Starting at the top of her head, glide one hand (either right or left) down your cat's back. When your hand is halfway down, start your other hand at the top, and begin that hand in its downward glide. As your first hand approaches the low back, glide it off, and continue again at the top. Repeat with your other hand, until you've created a wide, continuous loop from your two hands and Cat's back. Continue this in a constant, coordinated motion (which may take a bit of practice),

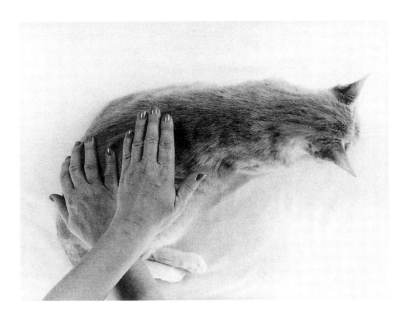

and find a comfortable rhythm. Some of these two-handed strokes can be long and flowing, with one glide covering the entire length of the back. Others can be shorter moves, with three glides to cover the back. Make them even smaller, and you'll fit six glides along her back. Think of maintaining a flowing, cascading motion. The two-handed approach makes this another marvelous technique. (This is so true. I just went over to Champion for practice so I could explain it. He craned his head in delight, twisted back to look at me, and flashed me a broad cat smile. This stuff works!)

CAUTION: Practice with two hands before you build up speed. For continuity, keep at least one hand on Cat at all times.

My Cat
Likes   _____

My Cat
Really Likes   _____

VARIATIONS: Just as you did with *The Grand Effleurage*, explore all pressures, speeds, and moods. Have fun!

Base Fiddling: Rump Ruffling

AREA: The rump part of Cat's back.
HAND PARTS: Four fingers, two fingers.
HAND POSITIONS: Horizontal, palm down.
MOTION: Waving.
SPEED: Slow-mo, leisurely, fast 'n frisky.
PRESSURE: Light, mild, deep.
MOOD: Gentle and relaxed, playful, frolicky fun.

TECHNIQUE: With a downward horizontal waving motion, stroke the lowest third of Cat's back (about 2–3 inches to the base of the tail). Use the flat part of your four fingers. Repeat this ruffle, back and forth, a few times. Concentrate on smooth repetition, and adjust your pressure, speed, and mood in response to Miss Kitty's feedback. Keep your strokes short while covering this area. During this stroke, many cats will raise up their rumps to meet your hand and express their pleasure. Often there's a slight slapping sound as your pinky finger slaps against the tail itself.

Some cats enjoy deep pressure at this point—so much so that it almost seems as if their legs will collapse under the weight of your hands.

My Cat
Likes   _____

My Cat
Really Likes   _____

CAUTION: There are some cats who do not enjoy this technique at all, and they will promptly let you know it. If so, abandon this one, and move on to the next one.

Ruffling Shuffle

AREA: Back.

HAND PARTS: Palm (open or closed), four fingers (open or closed), fingertips.

HAND POSITIONS: Horizontal, vertical, palm down.

MOTION: Waving, rubbing.

SPEED: Slow-mo, leisurely, fast 'n frisky.

PRESSURE: Light, mild.

MOOD: Gentle and relaxed, playful, frolicky fun.

TECHNIQUE: Now we'll work more of the back. With palm or four fingers, begin at the base of the neck, using a downward,

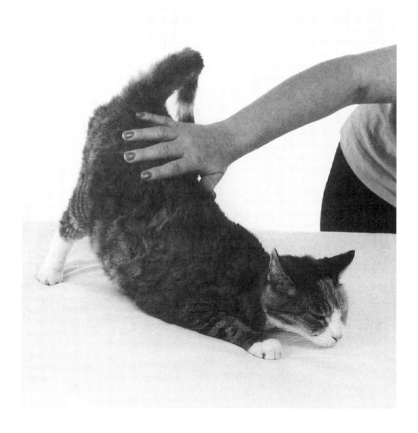

horizontal, ruffling wave for the first third of the back. Without stopping, reverse direction and stroke back up to your starting point, rubbing gently against the fur. Stroke further down again, and then back up, again and again. Keep this waving a fluid motion, gently flowing up and down the entire back. Repeat the stroke vertically, starting with your fingertips at the base of the neck, and your palm about one-third of the way down her back. Like a windshield wiper, ruffle some more. Keep that gentle rocking motion, and allow your cat to enjoy your artistry.

CAUTION: Afterward, make sure to unruffle the ruffled fur with hand, brush, or comb.

My Cat
Likes   _____

My Cat
Really Likes _____

Back Horseshoes

AREA: Length of back and top part of the sides of the cat.
HAND PARTS: Closed palm, four fingers.
HAND POSITIONS: Vertical, horseshoe.
MOTION: Gliding, circling.
SPEED: Slow-mo.
PRESSURE: Light.
MOOD: Gentle and relaxed.

TECHNIQUE: With Cat's permission, fit your horseshoe-shaped hand on her back, by her shoulders. Slowly glide your hand up and down, feeling your cat's body beneath your hand. Then move your hand further down along the spine a bit and continue this as you move down to the tail. Next, make circles with your fingers and follow down along the spine again.

ADVANCED TECHNIQUE: In a long gliding motion, with your hand in the horseshoe position, slide your hand along the length of the spine, from neck to rump, and then return up. Remember, return strokes always have lighter pressures.

My Cat
Likes   _____

My Cat
Really Likes   _____

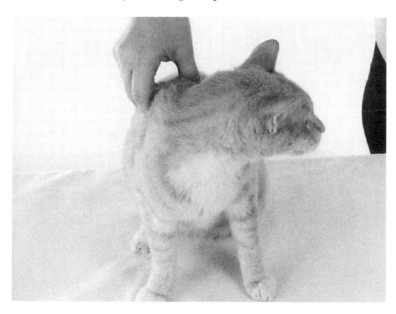

Spine Tingling

AREA: Back, from neck to rump.
HAND PART: Finger pads.
HAND POSITION: Vertical.
MOTION: Rubbing.
SPEED: Slow-mo.
MOOD: Gentle and relaxed, playful.

TECHNIQUE: Use the pads of your index and middle fingers. Position them on either side of the spine, and feel the bony vertebrae underneath. Slowly rub up and down *only* about an inch or so, move down an inch, and rub up and down again. Repeat until you've reached the tail, and work your way back up the same way. If Miss Kitty doesn't like her fur disturbed, this is not the technique for her.

CAUTION: For long nails, flatten fingers so that pads sink in, not the tips.

My Cat
Likes   _____

My Cat
Really Likes   _____

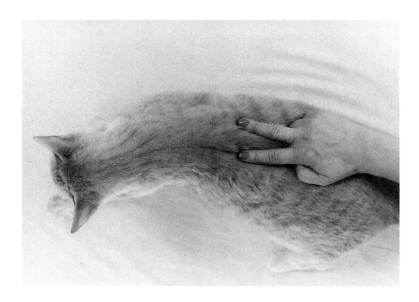

Alternate Circular Side Waving

AREA: Top and broad sides of Cat.

HAND PARTS: Palms (open or closed), finger pads, fingertips, four fingers.

HAND POSITION: Vertical.

MOTION: Circling, rubbing.

SPEED: Slow-mo, leisurely.

PRESSURE: Featherlight, light.

MOOD: Gentle and relaxed, playful.

TECHNIQUE: Create large clockwise and counterclockwise circles all over Cat, using two hands. You may also simply rub both hands up and down in unison.

CAUTION: Make sure she permits the fur ruffling that accompanies this technique. And always make sure that pressure is on a downward stroke only.

My Cat
Likes   _____

My Cat
Really Likes   _____

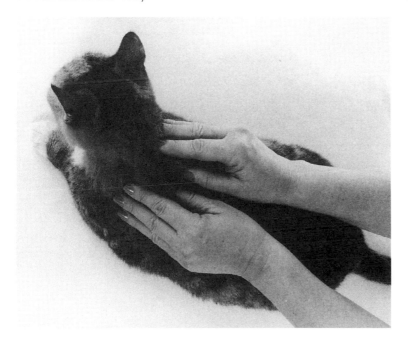

Farewell Flourishes

AREA: Back.
HAND PARTS: Finger pads, fingertips, four fingers, palm (open and closed).
HAND POSITIONS: Horizontal or vertical, palm down.
MOTION: Gliding.
SPEED: Slow-mo, leisurely.
PRESSURE: Featherlight, light, mild, deep.
MOOD: Gentle and relaxed, playful, frolicky fun.

My Cat
Likes   _____

My Cat
Really Likes   _____

TECHNIQUE: Gracious, glorious gliding motions that cascade along your cat's back. Make your speed smooth and calm, not rapid. Short and sweet, another simple and successful stroke, which can be a flourishing finale to any Cat Massage. Meow!

LET'S DO A LITTLE NECKING

Classic Pet: A Purr-ennial Favorite
Old-Fashioned Neck Scratching
Waving Down the Neckline
Cross-Neck Flicking
Occipital Bump Rubbing
Neck Horseshoes

Cats get neck pains, aches, or just plain muscle fatigue, just like people, so it's relaxing and beneficial to have their necks rubbed.

The cat's neck (top side) is supported by the first seven vertebrae of the spine. These bones are called the cervical vertebrae. At the top end, they attach directly to the cat's skull. At the lower end, they continue into the thoracic vertebrae, near the shoulder blades. Feel around here. The "bumps" you feel directly on the cat's spine are called the spinous processes. Each vertebrae also has a bony protuberance on each side called the transverse process. There's so much activity within the neck area, with a multitude of muscles, bones, tendons, nerves, and blood vessels involved. Relaxing massage work in this area has a soothing effect that your cat will feel all over.

Remember, when massaging this area, *never* apply deep pressure directly onto the spine. We never want to give or be a pain in the neck to our feline friend. So collect your cat, find a comfortable place, and let's do a little necking.

Classic Pet: A Purr-ennial Favorite

AREA: Top side of neck.
HAND PARTS: Four fingers, finger pads, fingertips.
HAND POSITIONS: Horizontal, palm down.
MOTION: Gliding.
SPEED: Slow-mo, leisurely, fast 'n frisky.
PRESSURE: Featherlight, light, mild, deep.

TECHNIQUE: This is a familiar neck stroke. Most of us instinctively rub a cat between the ears at the top of the neck. It's a common way to introduce ourselves to new cats. With your hand horizontal or vertical to Cat, glide lightly from neck to shoulders, with pressure on the down stroke only. A simple stroke, an excellent introductory move, and one that encourages immediate feline feedback indicating further massage. This is like a mini *Grand Effleurage*. Segue right into *Old-Fashioned Neck Scratching*.

My Cat
Likes   _____

My Cat
Really Likes   _____

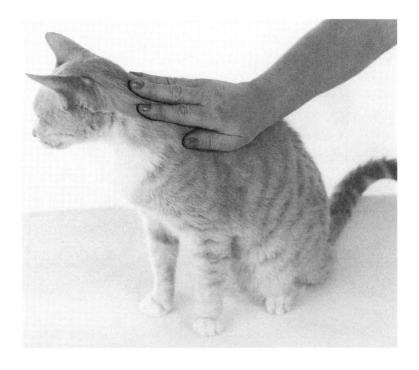

Old-Fashioned Neck Scratching

AREA: Top and sides of neck.
HAND PARTS: Finger pads, fingertips, thumb.
HAND POSITION: Vertical.
MOTION: Rubbing, flicking.
SPEED: Slow-mo, leisurely, fast 'n frisky.
PRESSURE: Featherlight, light, mild, deep.
MOOD: Gentle and relaxed, playful, frolicky fun.

TECHNIQUE: This is similar to *Classic Pet,* just change your hand parts and position slightly for a new technique. It's easy—just switch from four fingers to finger pads and fingertips, change direction from horizontal to vertical, and scratch away. Cover the top and the sides of the neck. As Cat enjoys this move, he'll press his neck up to match your hand pressure. This technique leads right into *Waving Down the Neckline*.

VARIATION: Add a rippling motion, like playing the flute. Begin with the pinky and end with the thumb.

My Cat
Likes   _____

My Cat
Really Likes   _____

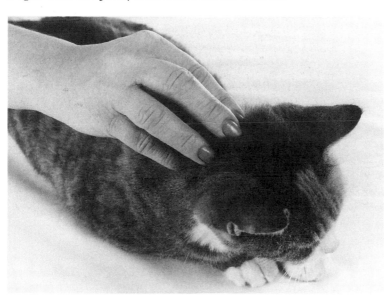

Waving Down the Neckline

AREA: Top and sides of neck, into the shoulder.
HAND PARTS: Finger pads, four fingers, Palm (open or closed).
HAND POSITION: Vertical.
MOTION: Waving.
SPEED: Slow-mo, leisurely, fast 'n frisky.
PRESSURE: Light, mild, deep.
MOOD: Gentle and relaxed, playful, frolicky fun.

TECHNIQUE: Place your hand in the vertical position, with fingers pointing toward Cat's head. Stroke sideways, like a windshield wiper, or like you're waving good-bye, and work your way down along the neck. Alternate short, half-inch waves, with longer waves. Let your gentle waves extend along the sides of Cat's neck, too, with as much pressure as she allows. Alternate this with *Old-Fashioned Neck Scratching*.

My Cat
Likes   _____

My Cat
Really Likes   _____

CAUTION: Be aware of the weight of your hand. Remember your cat's head is tiny in comparison to yours and be careful not to unintentionally press her head forward during this technique.

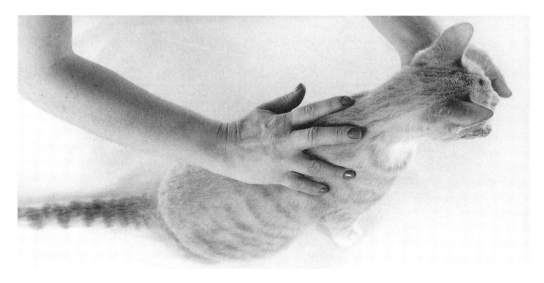

Cross-Neck Flicking

AREA: Neck.
HAND PARTS: Fingertips, open palm, four fingers.
HAND POSITION: Horizontal.
MOTION: Flicking.
SPEED: Slow-mo, leisurely.
PRESSURE: Featherlight, light.
MOOD: Gentle and relaxed, playful.

TECHNIQUE: Just like the *Apex Flicking* massage technique for the head (p. 50), stroke Cat's neck with a flicking motion across her spine. Work back and forth, moving up and down the length of the neck. This is a superficial stroke, with more emphasis on

fur rather than on bones and muscles. If you apply pressure to one side of the neck only, Cat will probably rub against you in responsive rhythm.

ADVANCED TECHNIQUE: Cup Cat's head on the base of your open palm, and let it rest there. Your palm will be supporting her head and your fingers will be free. Use them to reach out and stroke across her neck.

My Cat
Likes   _____

My Cat
Really Likes   _____

CAUTION: Again, remember how fragile Cat's neck is. Please do not press it forward during this technique. Also be careful not to scratch if you have longer nails.

Occipital Bump Rubbing

AREA: The occiput (bump) at the back of the Cat's head.
HAND PARTS: Finger pads, thumb pad, fingertips, four fingers.
HAND POSITIONS: Horizontal, vertical, cupping.
MOTION: Circling, waving, rubbing.
SPEED: Leisurely, fast 'n frisky.
PRESSURE: Featherlight, light, mild, deep.
MOOD: Gentle and relaxed, playful.

TECHNIQUE: Locate the bump at the back of Cat's head. Massage this occipital bump with one or more finger pads, or thumb pad, rotating in tiny clockwise and counterclockwise circles. Try fingertips for a precise feel, and four fingers for a broad approach. When doing precise fingertip work here, you can exert deeper

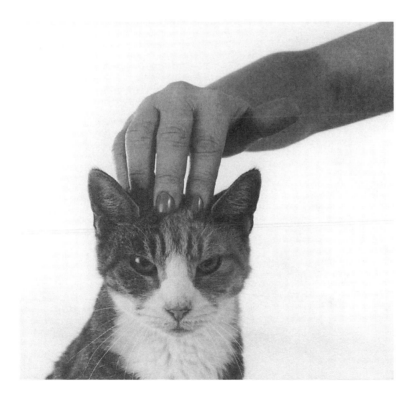

pressure, probing around the occiput. Or position your middle and ring fingers between the occiput, and gently wave back and forth. And of course, you can cover the area with small rubbing motions.

CAUTION: No flicking here, because it's bony, not soft.

My Cat
Likes   _____

My Cat
Really Likes   _____

VARIATION: As you massage the occiput with one hand, cup the chin in the other hand. This allows for deeper neck work, and Cat is more comfortable having her head supported.

Neck Horseshoes

AREA: Neck.
HAND PARTS: Closed palm, four fingers, thumb.
HAND POSITION: Horseshoe.
MOTION: Gliding, circling.
SPEED: Slow.
PRESSURE: Light, mild, deep.
MOOD: Gentle and relaxed, playful.

TECHNIQUE: Position your hand in the horseshoe with your thumb on one side of the neck, the web of your hand across the spine, and the four fingers on the other side of the neck. Pull hand up, in a light, gliding squeeze. Release pressure on

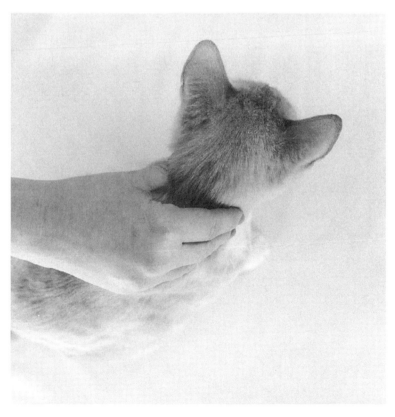

the down stroke and repeat a few times. Follow your cat's response. Now make small circles with all five fingers working
together.

CAUTION: Squeeze lightly, gently, never aggressively.

VARIATION: With your four fingers in the horseshoe position,
feel the bony structures within Cat's neck, and gently rotate
your fingers along those grooves. Then relax the pressure on that
side and use your thumb in the same way on the other side. As
you learn more quality massage in this area, you will be taking a
very positive role in relaxing your cat's neck.

My Cat
Likes   _____

My Cat
Really Likes _____

SCAPULA PLEASE: JUST BETWEEN US SHOULDER BLADES

Shoulder Strumming
Two-Finger Spine Slides
Two-handed Circular Shoulder Fanning
Just Between Us Shoulder Blades
Biceps-Triceps Touching
Underarm Tickle
Sinking into the Shoulders from Below

The shoulder joint is one of the busiest parts of your cat. Imagine it as a major intersection of muscles. Located between the shoulders, the scapula is a large, triangular, flat bone, with prominent ridges, crests, curves, and grooves. It acts as an anchor for the more than thirty muscles, tendons, and ligaments that function in the shoulder area. This is a busy and sophisticated muscular location, and is always in use, in some way, when your cat is moving.

The shoulder joint also bears the weight of the heaviest part of your cat—its front end. The intricate muscular design allows your cat its trademark agility and versatility. Much of a cat's movement is forward-backward motion, what we see when he walks or runs. But the shoulder joint's flexibility enables a cat to turn on a dime, to flip himself upright in a fall, or spread his legs wide. The strong shoulder joint also bears the impact when your cat lands on its paws in a leap from a table or windowsill.

Shoulder work will be an important part of your Cat Massage routine. Think for a moment of how good you feel when someone rubs your aching shoulders. Although most Cats' shoulders don't hurt from being hunched over a desk for hours every day, or performing heavy manual work, they do tire in their daily activities. Leaf pouncing, for example, does have a certain fatigue factor.

Massage in this area will start off gently and relaxed, as always. However, this area allows for deeper exploration, as you are invited to gently probe in and around this complex musculature. Pay special attention to the grooves between the spine and the scapula, and massage with an assortment of pressures, speeds, and moods. You can try some 'no-mo' techniques, cupping, and one-handed support-and-stroke work. And, since there are two shoulders, two-handed (bilateral) massage works well here.

Shoulder Strumming

AREA: Side of shoulder.
HAND PARTS: Finger pads, fingertips, four fingers.
HAND POSITIONS: Horizontal, vertical.
MOTION: Gliding, rubbing, waving.
SPEED: Slow-mo, leisurely, fast 'n frisky, no-mo.
PRESSURE: Light, mild, deep.
MOOD: Gentle and relaxed, playful, frolicky fun.

TECHNIQUE: Feel your cat's shoulders, and caress the area with a slow, downward gliding motion. Keep pressure on the de-

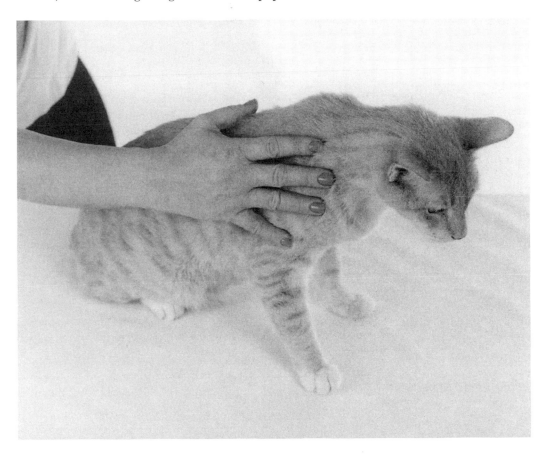

scending glide, and return back with a lighter rubbing touch. Notice the size and shape of the scapula, and feel for different crests and ridges. Then repeat with a waving, ruffling motion and faster speed. This technique is great whether Cat is standing, sitting, or on her side.

My Cat
Likes   _____

My Cat
Really Likes _____

ADVANCED TECHNIQUE: Let your fingers rest still (in no-mo) and let them sink into the shoulder area. Then, in slow-mo, trace the pattern of the scapula, and move ever so slowly over its bumpy curves.

Two-Finger Spine Slides

AREA: Neck, from the base of the skull down to the shoulder
   blades.
HAND PART: Finger pads.
HAND POSITION: Vertical.
MOTION: Gliding.
SPEED: Slow-mo.
PRESSURE: Light, mild, deep.
MOOD: Gentle and relaxed, playful, frolicky fun.

TECHNIQUE: Use your index and middle finger pads only. Position them on either side of the spine, resting them in the groove
along the vertebrae (the spine). Begin near the base of the head
and slide your finger pads down the cervical spine to the shoul-

der blades. Let your fingers sink into this area. Probe deeper—if Cat allows—and explore specific areas carefully. This technique always goes with the grain . . . tailward.

My Cat
Likes   _____

My Cat
Really Likes   _____

CAUTION: If your nails are long, flatten your fingers so that your finger pads sink in, not the tips.

Two-handed Circular Shoulder Fanning

AREA: Shoulder area.

HAND PARTS: Finger pads, fingertips, four fingers, palms (open or closed).

HAND POSITIONS: Horizontal, vertical.

MOTION: Rubbing, circling.

SPEED: Leisurely.

PRESSURE: Mild.

MOOD: Gentle and relaxed, playful.

TECHNIQUE: Using the different hand parts, rub up and down in a strumming motion, or massage clockwise and counterclockwise circles along both of the shoulders. Rotate your hands simultaneously or in alternating rhythm. The beauty in this stroke is in using two hands for a doubly good feeling.

ADVANCED TECHNIQUE: This is a really groovy move. With Cat facing you, hook the four fingertips of both hands (index through pinky) along the groove of the spine and scapula, allowing your hands to drape down across the shoulders. In this position, your palms will be resting on the shoulders and your fingers will be sinking a bit deeply into the muscular shoulder area. The weight of this position can separate the shoulder blades *ever so slightly*. With hands positioned comfortably, rotate your fingers along the scapula ridge, and then rub the shoulder blades with the base of your palms.

My Cat
Likes   _____

My Cat
Really Likes   _____

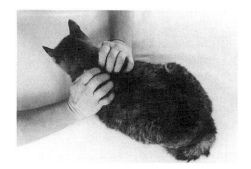

Just Between Us Shoulder Blades

AREA: Ridge between shoulder blades and spine.
HAND PARTS: Finger pads, fingertips.
HAND POSITION: Palm down.
MOTION: Flicking, rubbing, circling.
SPEED: Slow-mo, leisurely.
PRESSURE: Light, mild, deep.
MOOD: Gentle and relaxed.

TECHNIQUE: This area is best approached with Cat in front of you or at your side. Slide one finger down from the back of the head/neck to the ridge between the shoulder blades. Feel the complex arrangement of muscles, tendons, and ligaments, and work your finger pads gently in and among the area. You may also use the fingertips of one, two, three, or four fingers. Massage back and forth, side to side, and create circles over this active area.

My Cat
Likes   _____

My Cat
Really Likes   _____

CAUTION: Make sure this area is warmed up with gentle stroking before you massage, and very warmed up before you probe deeper.

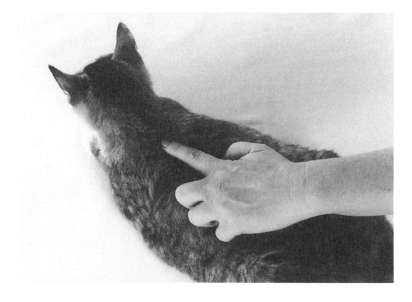

Biceps-Triceps Touching

AREA: Upper part of the front leg, extending into the shoulder.
HAND PARTS: Finger pads, fingertips, two fingers.
HAND POSITIONS: Horizontal, horseshoe.
MOTION: Rubbing.
SPEED: Slow-mo.
PRESSURE: Light, mild.
MOOD: Gentle and relaxed.

TECHNIQUE: Gently stroke along Cat's muscular front leg, from shoulder to paw and back. Rub below the fur, and if allowed, add a few gentle squeezes. Simple light scratching also feels good here.

ADVANCED TECHNIQUE: Hold the upper foreleg in the horseshoe position, and with the index and middle fingers together, thumb extended on the other side, rub back and forth, and gently squeeze.

My Cat
Likes   _____
My Cat
Really Likes _____

Underarm Tickle

AREA: Armpit.
HAND PARTS: Finger pads, fingertips.
HAND POSITION: Palm down.
MOTION: Rubbing.
SPEED: Slow-mo.
PRESSURE: Light, mild.
MOOD: Gentle and relaxed, playful.

TECHNIQUE: This is best done when Cat is lying on his back or side. When your cat is favorably involved with shoulder massage, he is ready for the *Underarm Tickle*. Massage in and around the shoulder and chest areas, and weave your way up to the armpit. With his front leg extended, stroke back and forth in this area (listen closely for cat giggles). If Cat lets you, use your fingertips for light scratching, bestowing upon your cat a most unexpected, amusing delight. Sometimes your other hand can help out, gently lifting his extended leg back, and giving you more area to massage. At other times, your cat's pleasure will be obvious—widespread front legs reaching out, telling you that you've done it right again! When done correctly, this technique is sure to produce a cat smile!

My Cat
Likes   _____

My Cat
Really Likes   _____

Sinking Into the Shoulders from Below

AREA: Ridge between the spine and shoulder blades, on the
  top side of Cat.
HAND PARTS: Finger pads, fingertips.
HAND POSITION: Cupping.
MOTION: Rubbing.
SPEED: Slow-mo, leisurely.
PRESSURE: Light, mild.
MOOD: Gentle and relaxed.

TECHNIQUE: When Cat is lying on his back, reach your fingers
underneath his body. Cat may be skeptical at first, but patience

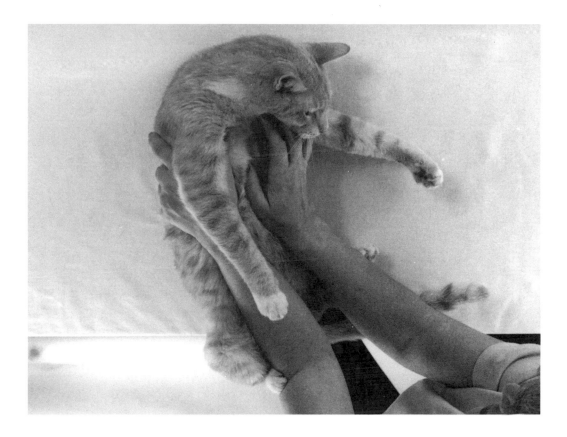

My Cat
Likes   _____

My Cat
Really Likes   _____

pays with this technique. Feel for the groove between the spine and the scapula, and maneuver your finger pads and fingertips along those muscles. With the added weight of your cat's own body, let your fingers sink up into the shoulders, and gently work this area from a new perspective. Gentle rocking motions here are wonderful, and your cat may add to the pleasure by shifting his body weight to maximize the massage. This technique is also fun simply because it's such a novel way of approaching your cat. The beauty of this technique is in the approach from below, when Cat is lying on his back. (If your cat is not on his back, save this technique for another time.)

TREASURE CHEST

Breast Stroking
Buffing the Breastplate
Chest Cupping
Petting the Pecs

The front of your cat is a veritable treasure chest that is easily accessible, and often acceptable from a cat's point of view. Head, neck, and shoulder massage all naturally point to the chest as the next Cat Massage location. This in turn makes the Treasure Chest a natural lead-in to Side Stroking. Many strokes here encourage cat stretching, particularly the kind of stretching where your cat rolls onto his back or side and shows off his beautiful furry chest and tummy. The chest can be approached from the front or from the side, especially when you are holding your cat. This area generates interesting feedback.

Breast Stroking

AREA: Chest.
HAND PARTS: Finger pads, fingertips, four fingers.
HAND POSITIONS: Horizontal, vertical.
MOTION: Waving.
SPEED: Slow-mo, leisurely, fast 'n frisky.
PRESSURE: Light, deep.
MOOD: Gentle and relaxed, playful, frolicky fun.

TECHNIQUE: Simply wave your way around Cat's furry front. When your cat raises his head to give you more petting room, take that as a friendly-feedback signal and continue. Then you can do some detailed touch using your fingertips to strum. Horizontally work your way from the top of Cat's throat down to and in and around his chest and under his arms. Then vertically wave across both shoulders. Begin leisurely and light, then build up to fast 'n frisky and use deeper pressure—with Cat's permission.

ADVANCED TECHNIQUE: Let Cat's head rest on your palm and thumb, and scratch with four fingers.

My Cat
Likes   _____

My Cat
Really Likes _____

CAUTION: Be careful to not press the throat on an upswing, or press too deeply on his windpipe.

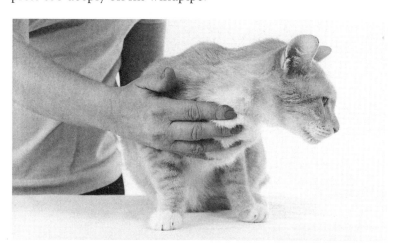

Buffing the Breastplate

AREA: Center of chest, the bump of his breastplate (sternum).
HAND PARTS: Finger pads, four fingers.
HAND POSITIONS: Cupping, horizontal.
MOTION: Rubbing, waving.
PRESSURE: Featherlight, light, mild.
SPEED: Slow-mo, leisurely.
MOOD: Gentle and relaxed, playful.

TECHNIQUE: Feel the bony protuberance on the front of Cat's chest, in the center of his breastplate. Rub in and around this area—a simple technique. Add some gentle waving if desired.

My Cat
Likes   _____

My Cat
Really Likes   _____

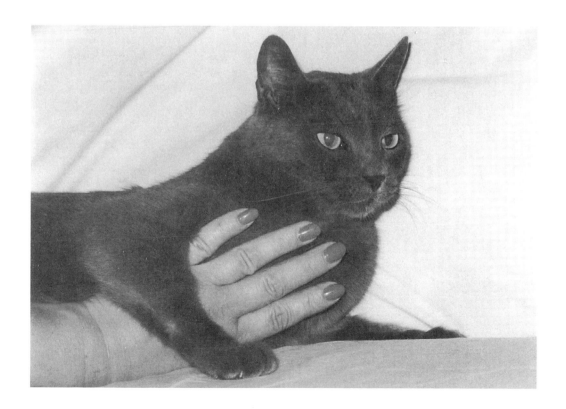

Chest Cupping

AREA: Chest.
HAND PART: Palm (open or closed).
HAND POSITION: Cupping.
MOTION: None.
SPEED: No-mo, slow-mo.
PRESSURE: Light.
MOOD: Gentle and relaxed.

My Cat
Likes   _____

My Cat
Really Likes   _____

TECHNIQUE: In this technique, simply cup Cat's chest in your palm. Then, hold it still for a short while. This is time to be together, to breathe together, feeling your Cat's chest rise and fall. Then add a slight squeeze for variation, but this is primarily a no-mo technique. Allow your cat's chin to rest on your hand, and just spend a few peaceful moments like this.

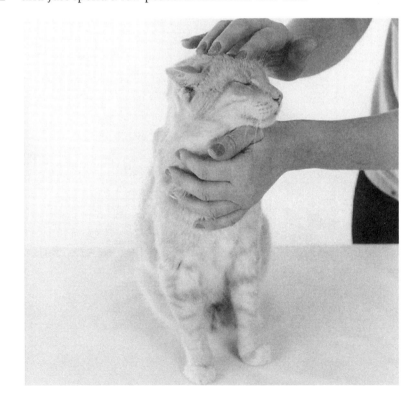

Petting the Pecs

AREA: Pectoral muscle on the front of Cat's chest, in and
around the shoulder blades.
HAND PARTS: Palm (open or closed), finger pads, fingertips.
HAND POSITION: Horizontal.
MOTION: Rubbing.
SPEED: Slow-mo, leisurely.
PRESSURE: Light, mild.
MOOD: Gentle and relaxed, playful.

TECHNIQUE: When Cat is in position to expose his chest, help
him out by rubbing in and around the mighty pectoral muscles.
(These are the prominent muscles seen on the chest of proud
bodybuilders.) When your hand is in position, let your palm rest
lightly on his chest and massage this area. You can even draw his
front leg back *ever so slightly* for more massaging area.

My Cat
Likes   _____

My Cat
Really Likes   _____

SIDE STROKING

Light Fur Fluffing: A Subtle Satisfying Surprise
Cat Sandwich
Four-Finger Fanning
Layla's Luxurious Front-Paw to Back-Claw Caress

Conjure an image of a relaxing cat. It will often be that of a cat reclining on its side. Lying on one side exposes quite a large amount of body surface area, and invites a multitude of mellow massage work, especially long, luxurious stroking.

Now that your capable hands have learned strokes for the head, neck, shoulders, and chest of your favorite feline, it's time to learn how to massage the side of his body as well. With some minor adjustments, the Back for More strokes work equally as well on the side. The movements here are very gentle and relaxed. Side Stroking is often a prelude to Tummy Touching. Since it is a position of comfort, many cats who start their massage standing or sitting, will often finish lying on their side.

Light Fur Fluffing: A Subtle Satisfying Surprise

AREA: Side of Cat.
HAND PARTS: Finger pads, fingertips, four fingers, palm (open or closed).
HAND POSITION: Palm down.
MOTION: Gliding.
SPEED: Slow-mo.
PRESSURE: Featherlight.
MOOD: Gentle and relaxed.

TECHNIQUE: Easy does it here. This technique is full of graceful, flowing caresses. Just like its name, emphasis is on the very tender touch. Keep pressure featherlight and speed very slow. Follow the contours of Cat's body, from shoulder to shank, gliding only tailward.

My Cat
Likes   _____

My Cat
Really Likes   _____

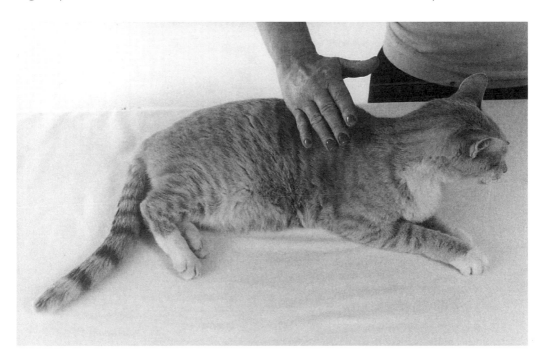

Cat Sandwich

AREA: Both sides of Cat.
HAND PART: Palms (open or closed).
HAND POSITION: Palms (up and down).
MOTION: Gliding.
SPEED: Slow-mo.
PRESSURE: Light.
MOOD: Gentle and relaxed.

My Cat
Likes   _____

My Cat
Really Likes   _____

TECHNIQUE: Position one hand under Cat's body at the shoulder. Put your other hand on top of the corresponding shoulder that is facing you, with Cat in the middle. Slide your hands slowly down along both sides of your cat, from shoulders and chest to rump. Continue out to the tip of the tail.

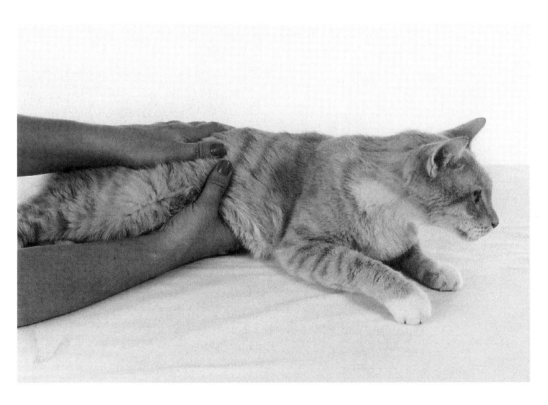

Four-Finger Fanning

AREA: From shoulder down entire length of body.
HAND PARTS: Thumb, four fingers.
HAND POSITION: Horizontal.
MOTION: Gliding, waving.
SPEED: Slow-mo, leisurely.
PRESSURE: Featherlight.
MOOD: Gentle and relaxed.

TECHNIQUE: Start with your thumb anchored by the shoulder and use it as a point of rotation. If your cat is lying on her left side, use your left thumb; if Cat is on her right side, anchor with your right thumb. Let your four fingers rest on Cat, index finger closer to the head, pinky finger nearer the tail, and allow them to glide and wave across the area formed by this arc. Use featherlight pressure on the downward arc, and no pressure at all on the return move.

My Cat
Likes   _____

My Cat
Really Likes   _____

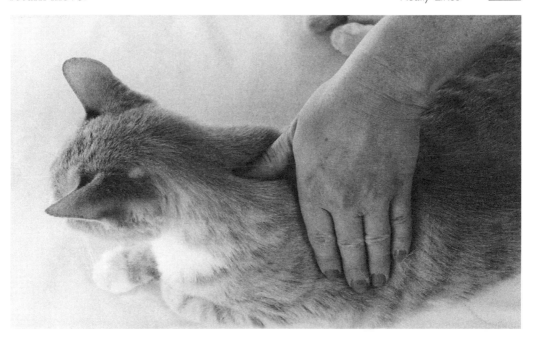

Layla's Luxurious Front-Paw to Back-Claw Caress

AREA: Entire side of Cat, from front paw to back claw.
HAND PARTS: Four fingers, palm (open or closed).
HAND POSITION: Vertical.
MOTION: Gliding.
SPEED: Slow-mo, leisurely.
PRESSURE: Light.
MOOD: Gentle and relaxed.

TECHNIQUE: This technique works when Cat is lying completely stretched out on her side. (Isn't it amazing how far they can stretch like this?) Begin at the very tip of her front paws, and slowly begin one long, flowing glide. Continue on the foreleg, along the shoulder, side, back, down her thigh, lower foreleg, and end at her back claws. Do not glide back up her body. Take all the time in the world with this technique—the slower the better. Sometimes, just when you think your cat can't grow any longer, she'll stretch out a few more inches in glorious response and appreciation of this luxurious caress. It's a great touch.

My Cat
Likes   _____

My Cat
Really Likes   _____

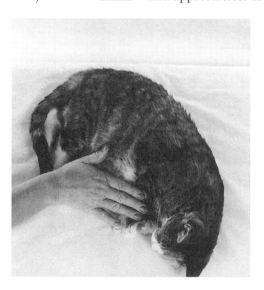
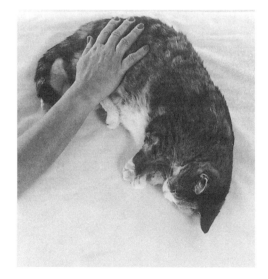

TUMMY TOUCHING

Belly Browsing
Four-Paws Belly-Up Spread
Stand-Up Stomach Stroking

The belly can be a very indecisive area. Some days massage is desired here, and other days it's hands-off territory. Cats are very sensitive and finicky here. It's that simple. But if your cat is ready, willing, and desiring, go for it.

How do you know if your cat will go belly up for some Tummy Touching? When purrs encourage you to continue. If she growls, this may be a warning that the belly is off-limits—a belly-bomber day. Every cat will sometimes have them. Determine belly-bomber days using the same feline feedback that work for other cat parts. Be quicker to notice and respond, because some cats may draw claws here.

The best belly work begins at the chest level, weaving your way down to the tummy area. Avoid starting off low on the abdomen—even a well-massaged mouser appreciates warm-up work here. Keep the speed slow, pressure light, and mood gentle and relaxed. So, on desirable days, here's what to do for some abdominal action.

Belly Browsing

AREA: Belly.

HAND PARTS: Palm (open or closed), four fingers, finger pads, fingertips.

HAND POSITIONS: Vertical or horizontal.

MOTION: Rubbing, circling.

SPEED: Slow-mo.

PRESSURE: Featherlight, light.

MOOD: Gentle and relaxed.

TECHNIQUE: First use the techniques in the Treasure Chest (pp. 93–97) to introduce yourself to this area. Begin at the chest level with Cat lying on his side or back. Very lightly and very slowly begin rubbing, ruffling, and caressing the belly area. Feel around the belly, reach around to the sides as well, and find out what Cat fancies.

My Cat
Likes   _____

My Cat
Really Likes   _____

ADVANCED TECHNIQUE: For "clockwise cuddling," make wide circles around Cat's belly and alternate with smaller ones. Although your pressure will be featherlight, this clockwise movement technically helps to facilitate digestion. And it's soothing, like when a Mommy rubs her baby's tummy.

Four-Paws Belly-Up Spread

AREA: Belly.
HAND PARTS: Thumbs, four fingers.
HAND POSITION: Palms down.
MOTION: Rubbing.
SPEED: Slow-mo.
PRESSURE: Featherlight, light.
MOOD: Gentle and relaxed.

TECHNIQUE: As you pet your cat's belly, *gently and slowly* spread his four paws apart with your wrists and forearms. When his arms and legs are separated, and his belly exposed, lightly rub this area with your thumbs and four fingers.

CAUTION: This is a very advanced stroke so take your time. With patience and practice, combine this with the *Underarm Tickle* (p. 90).

My Cat
Likes   _____

My Cat
Really Likes   _____

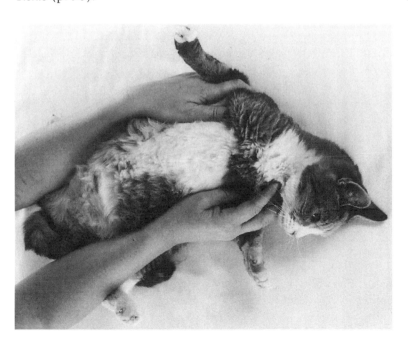

Stand-Up Stomach Stroking

AREA: Belly.
HAND PARTS: Finger pads, fingertips, four fingers, closed palm.
HAND POSITION: Palm up.
MOTION: Rubbing.
SPEED: Slow-mo.
PRESSURE: Light, mild.
MOOD: Gentle and relaxed.

TECHNIQUE: With Cat standing on all fours, feel his belly. Randomly rub your finger parts or closed palm from side to side, reaching in and around the legs. If Cat allows, increase to mild pressure, but keep the speed slow-mo. Definitely make sure Cat is warmed up before you try this. It's an unusual technique, an unusual position, and yet it generates the usual Cat Massage response—pleasant acceptance.

My Cat
Likes   ——

My Cat
Really Likes   ——

CAUTION: I tried this stroke after many years of Cat Massaging Champion. Unlike others, this stroke has an unpredictable outcome. Do not be surprised if your cat declines it. And if not—here's another one to add to your list!

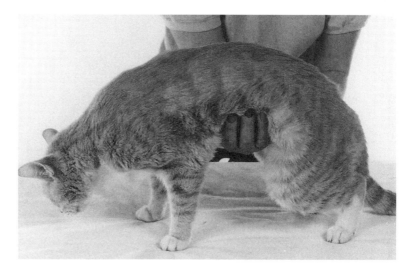

PAWS AND CLAWS

Paw-Claw Caress
Paw Press
Paw-Pad Press
Tiptoeing Through the Toes

They walk on them, they run with them, they climb up trees (and hopefully not your furniture) with them. They are used to viciously tear apart prey (again, hopefully not your furniture), yet they can shred tissue paper with comic, playful delight. These are the paws and claws of your cat.

The two front legs are called forelegs, and they hold the equivalent of our wrists, palms, and fingers (digits). The two back legs are called hindlegs (remember the hindleg maneuver) and they hold the equivalent of our ankles, soles, and toes (digits). At the end of each digit is a claw. Paw pads are also called tori. These friction pads form the cushioned surfaces on the bottom of your cat's feet. There are seven tori on the front paws, and five on the back paws.

The paws and claws are very sensitive areas of a Cat, and it takes finesse and constant reaffirming approval to massage this area. Please! No pulling their digits. It is not soothing, and you will so be informed. Better to hear it from me than from your cat—or more accurately, from your cat's claws. Remember this: they knead to show they're pleased, they swat to show they're not. Note: All these techniques work just as well for declawed cats as for cats with claws. Declawed cats simply have mushier finger pads.

Paw-Claw Caress

AREA: Paw pad and claw.
HAND PARTS: Finger pads, thumb pad.
HAND POSITION: Palm up.
MOTION: Circling, rubbing.
SPEED: No-mo, slow-mo.
PRESSURE: Featherlight, light.
MOOD: Gentle and relaxed.

TECHNIQUE: With your finger pads or thumb pad facing upward, allow Cat's paw pad to rest on them. Let the paw rest there for a few moments to develop familiarity. Then slowly rotate your finger pads in clockwise or counterclockwise circles to feel the entire area of the paw pad. Or rub back and forth from the tip of the claw up to your cat's "wrist."

My Cat
Likes   _____

My Cat
Really Likes   _____

CAUTION: This a gentle area, so keep the approach and the massage gentle.

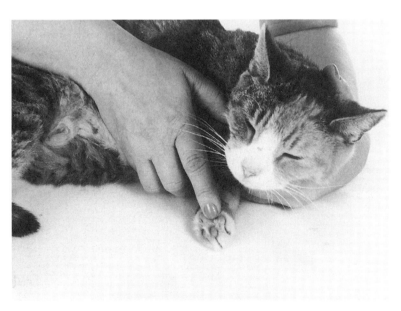

Paw Press

AREA: Paw, top and bottom.
HAND PARTS: Open palm, finger pads, thumb pad.
HAND POSITION: Cupping.
MOTION: None, kneading.
SPEED: No-mo, slow-mo.
PRESSURE: Featherlight.
MOOD: Gentle and relaxed.

TECHNIQUE: Gently enclose Cat's paw within your own "paw." Hold for a moment, and let her get accustomed to this new feel. Add a featherlight kneading squeeze, gauging her response before you continue. If allowed, you can even slowly rotate your hand around her paw, twisting back and forth, or slowly up and down. Just a new feel for a familiar area. Your cat will hand it to you—this is an interesting move.

CAUTION: If Cat agrees, fine—if not, don't take it personally—move onto another technique.

My Cat
Likes   _____

My Cat
Really Likes   _____

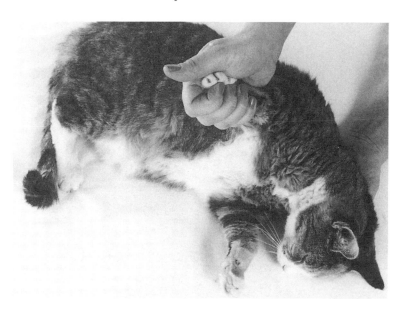

Paw-Pad Press

AREA: Paw pad.
HAND PARTS: Thumb, finger pads, thumb pad.
HAND POSITION: Cupping.
MOTION: Rubbing.
SPEED: Slow-mo.
PRESSURE: Light.
MOOD: Gentle and relaxed.

TECHNIQUE: Support the paw pad of Cat's front or back leg with your finger pads. Make a tiny "paw sandwich" with your index and middle finger pads together, facing up, your cat's paw in the middle, facing up or down, and your thumb pad on top, facing down. Gently and lightly rub her paw pad. If allowed, add a gentle squeeze. If Miss Kitty is declawed, feel around this area and *gently* move her paw to look at her paw pads. If Miss Kitty has claws, just make sure to get permission before attempting this. Pressing on the pad extends the claws, so you may even be encouraged to feel them, too. With practice, this can become a very interesting, exploring technique.

My Cat
Likes   _____

My Cat
Really Likes   _____

CAUTION: Go easy in this area, and follow Cat's lead.

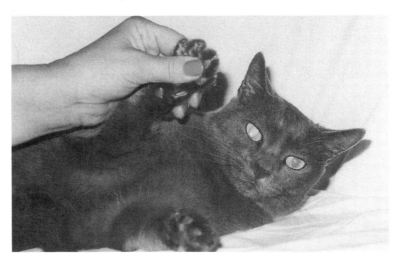

Tiptoeing Through the Toes

AREA: Toes.
HAND PARTS: Thumb, finger sides.
HAND POSITION: Palm down.
MOTION: Rubbing.
SPEED: Slow-mo.
PRESSURE: Light.
MOOD: Gentle and relaxed.

TECHNIQUE: After warming up with the previous massages, you can approach this detailed technique with confidence. Cat has relaxed and knows she's in good hands with you—so when she gives you her paw freely, feel in and among the individual toes on both her front and hindlegs. Using the sides of your thumb and index finger, slowly weave your way from the base of her toes out to their tips, or slowly follow each toe up and down, from pinky to thumb. For variety, move in around her paw pads.

CAUTION: As with each technique and with each variation, get Cat's permission before continuing.

My Cat
Likes   _____

My Cat
Really Likes   _____

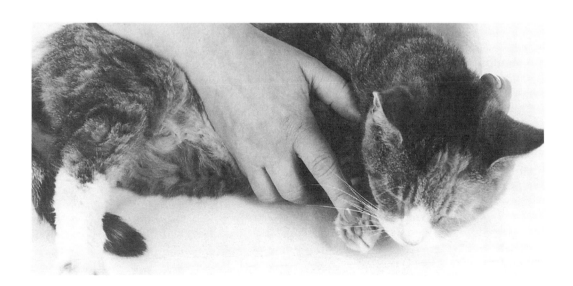

TAIL END

Caudal Cuddling
Tail End

In the wild jungle, the lion displays his magnificent mane as a badge of honor. At home, our domesticated feline is equally proud of his furry finale—his tail. Whether fat and fluffy, sleek and flowing, or, in the case of the Manx, practically nonexistent, a cat's tail is his badge of honor. Hours of grooming make this furry showpiece a display of distinction for the household cat.

The cat's tail corresponds to our coccyx bone; these bones are called the caudal vertebrae. Man has three to five bones fused together to form the coccyx; the cat has twenty-one to twenty-five caudal vertebrae that extend out to become the tail. This is literally the tail end of the vertebral column, but it's by no means the tail end of Cat Massage.

Caudal Cuddling

AREA: Tail.
HAND PARTS: Finger pads, thumb.
HAND POSITION: Horseshoe.
MOTION: Rubbing.
SPEED: Slow-mo, leisurely.
PRESSURE: Mild.
MOOD: Gentle and relaxed.

TECHNIQUE: Start from the base of the rump, and feel along the tail, right out to the tip. With the tail positioned between your four fingers and thumb, gently rub the tail and follow it out to its natural conclusion. You may add a gentle squeeze here if Cat allows.

CAUTION: This is tender territory; Cat may gracefully decline attention here.

My Cat
Likes   _____

My Cat
Really Likes   _____

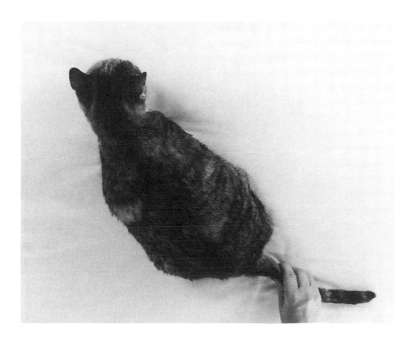

Tail End

AREA: Tail.
HAND PARTS: Finger pads, open palm, four fingers, thumb.
HAND POSITION: Palm down.
MOTION: Gliding.
SPEED: Slow-mo, leisurely.
PRESSURE: Featherlight, light.
MOOD: Gentle and relaxed.

My Cat
Likes   _____

My Cat
Really Likes   _____

TECHNIQUE: This is best done as an extension of *The Grand Effleurage* (see pp. 59–60). Follow the long gliding stroke right down to the rump and continue out to the tail. Lightly hold the tail in your hand with finger pads and open palm, or four fingers with thumb support, and gracefully glide tailward out to its tip. A farewell flourish, this is a most elegant finishing touch.

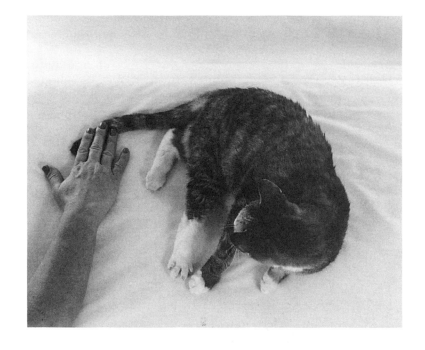

Voice Massage

🐾 There's an entirely unique style of Cat Massage that involves no touching at all—simply talking. Sometimes when Champion is resting comfortably (which is usually eighteen to twenty hours a day), I'll go over to him and quietly talk, in a gentle whisper. This verbal caress starts a whole new response, and it's most interesting. Voice Massage came about when my arms were tucked in under blankets and didn't want to come out, or when Champion was tucked in a nook or cranny, and I was unable to reach him, but I still wanted to communicate with him—so I talked to him. The results were amazingly similar to actual Cat Massage touching and the feline feedback was just as positive. Voilà! Voice Massage!

Perhaps you are already incorporating Voice Massage with your cat. Do you ever find yourself talking to your cat? Can you keep a dialogue punctuated with meows from your feline friend? Welcome to the world of Voice Massage! It's the quality of your particular voice that becomes so familiar, so friendly, so reassuring, and eventually so desirable.

Cat conversation ranges from cat-calling coos to complete verbal exchanges. Cat-calling coos are actually cues for interaction and bonding. The two most common ones are most obscure to define on paper, but you'll surely recognize them, so here they are. The first sound is as if you're sucking on a straw, or a long strand of spaghetti, but with your lips closed tightly. Either a long "mmmmccchhhh" or a short, staccato "mmcchh," sound fills the air. Recognize it? The other sound is the "ssswwwsss-ssswwwsss"—as if you're saying the word "Swiss" without the vowel. You often see people calling a cat this way, with their mouth and cheeks in full activity. I do hope you followed this, because Champion sure did—every time I'd practice explaining a sound, he'd come over to me.

Your cat will appreciate the soothing rhythmic pattern you develop together, and it can become a lullaby of sorts. All the telltale friendly feline-feedback signals will appear—the purring, the air-kneading paws, and, of course, the cat smile. Another massage well done!

White-Glove Treatments: Special Massage Medleys for Your Special Cat

Triple Delight

Crowning the King/Queen.
The Grand *Effleurage*.
Check Out Those Cheeks.

Good-Morning Massage Medley

Crowning the King/Queen.
Old-Fashioned Neck Scratching.
Breast Stroking.
Two-Finger Spine Slides.
Four-Finger Fanning.
Paw-Pad Press.
Biceps-Triceps Touching.
Neck Horseshoes.
Chinny Chin Chin.

Long Luxurious Caresses

These are great techniques to begin or end a massage: they establish a peaceful tone and environment. When a calm, soothing massage is desired, try:

Classic Pet.
The Grand *Effleurage*.
Layla's Luxurious Front-Paw to Back-Claw Caress.
Hand Over Hand and Down We Go.

In fact, try any Cat Massage, just slower.

Rushed and Running Out the Door

These are last-minute marvelous massages, for when your intentions are good, but the timing is bad. Work on larger areas, like the back and shoulder. Make it vigorous, building up to fast 'n frisky speeds, and deeper pressures. Cover twice as much with two hands, and Voice Massage—explain to Cat that you'll be back for more.

The Grand *Effleurage*.
Shoulder Strumming.
Ruffling Shuffle.
Base Fiddling.
Waving Down the Neckline.
Side of the Head Stroking: Champion's Favorite.

Nighty-Night Nuzzling

These are slow movements focusing on the face, head, and neck, or involve long, slow back strokes. This area is a major sensory center, and a good place for bedtime touching. *Francesca's Fore-head Favorite* (p. 51) became her favorite during these evening sessions. *Chin-Ups* (pp. 47–48) is a great way to settle down, and *Light Fur Fluffing* (p. 99) may be your last stroke before sleep.

Dynamic Duo

Chin-Ups (pp. 47–48) and *Side of the Head Stroking* (p. 55) (using knuckle nooks) is a partnership of techniques that make for a long, lasting partnership for you and your cat. It is Champion's and my most favorite massage medley.

White-Glove Treatments

Special gloves create different textures. Basic winter gloves work well—so do mittens—they give a different feel to our massages. Thin driving gloves and very-thin cotton gloves from photography supply stores work just fine. You wear the gloves—not Cat!

Brush Massage

Daily brushing with a bristle brush is recommended for your cat to remove extra fur, help with grooming, and keep the coat well oiled. Cat Massage techniques make your brushing routines tolerable for some cats, and thoroughly enjoyable for others. Use the same guidelines—follow the contours of Cat, and begin slowly and patiently, with light pressure, and get creative. There's more fun to this necessary health regimen than you'd ever expect when you combine it with Cat Massage.

These are great Cat Massage combinations. By now you've realized that the best massage medleys will be the ones you both create—like these:

_____

_____

_____

_____

Catastrophes to Avoid: The No-No's of Cat Massage

Just about everything about Cat Massage is positive: any drawbacks are outweighed by the positives. To keep it that way, I've listed a few reminders of what *not* to do during Cat Massage. Hopefully they're quite obvious.

- Never force a massage on a cat. It absolutely won't work and Cat will end up frustrated and angry.
- If you're not in a good mood, don't massage. You'll end up frustrated and angry.
- No oils, creams, or lotions are necessary—just your clean hands.
- *Absolutely never* give a cat any kind of massage if you are under the influence of alcohol or drugs. Your perception would be altered more than you'd think, and the results could be disastrous or downright devastating to your cat.
- Never pull Cat's fur, ears, or tail. Just like Mom says: "Would you like someone to do that to you?" I think not, so don't do it to your cat.
- Never pull Cat's whiskers. This applies especially to children or adults who think this is cute. It is not.
- Never press on Cat's stomach. You can easily damage internal organs.

- Massage with your hands, *not* your feet, no matter how comfortable you are with this, or how long you've been massaging. This is a potential hazard just waiting to happen, and I don't advocate it, *ever*.
- A cat's private parts are just that—private—to be left alone and not to be touched by you during massage.
- Never press too deeply on your cat. You'll avoid what "too deeply" is if you start off lightly and follow your cat's responses. Remember that we are so much bigger and stronger than our felines.
- Watch your fingernails! Long beautiful nails belong on a lovely hand, but they can only be used for Cat Massage when used properly. Be *extra* careful with *all* techniques, especially near sensitive or delicate areas such as the ears and whiskers.
- Never substitute massage for veterinary treatment. If you are massaging a postoperative or ailing cat, do so *only* with the awareness and approval of your cat's doctor.
- Be careful to not rush too much too soon. It's a tempting human trait to run through and show off everything you've just learned, but don't do this—you'll exhaust your poor pet. While learning Cat Massage, keep variety to a minimum. Hopefully, you and your cat will be together for quite a while, so gracefully take your time and enjoy all that Cat Massage has to offer.

Tips to Remember for Cat Massage

- If you like cats, you'll adore Cat Massage.
- Petting makes friends, but massage makes partners.
- Honor your cat's responses and respect boundaries.
- This book is meant to be suggestive only. If you are thorough from the start, you'll be amazed at the friendly feedback you'll receive.
- Variety is the spice of Cat Massage.
- Practice with patience and perfect with persistence.
- Cat Massage is therapy—sometimes for Cat, sometimes for you.
- Cats' belief system is centered in the knowledge that they are running the show at all times. Help them maintain their feline superiority theory.
- Your primary purpose when Cat Massaging is the well-being and comfort of your cat.
- Cats knead to show they're pleased, they swat to show they're not.
- With Cat Massage, payback is a pleasure.
- Massage feels good and is good for you, whether "you" happens to be the human or the cat.
- When your cat kneads you, you'll know she really needs you.

- Occasionally return to basics—update and refresh your techniques.
- Practice and patience make perfect Cat Massage technique.
- Pet a cat, you make a friend for a day. Massage a cat, you make a friend for life.
- Although it is necessary to always start in a gentle and relaxed mood, it's not always necessary to go faster. Remember, a good massage starts slow and finishes fast. A great massage starts slow and finishes slow.
- It's not what's right or wrong, it's what works.
- Enjoy, enjoy, enjoy!

Special Considerations

The Beauty of Youth: Kittens and Kids
The Wisdom of Age: Senior Stroking
Let's Mention Mommy: Pregnant Cats
Ailing and Recuperating: Cats and People

The Beauty of Youth: Kittens and Kids

After cats, kittens are surely the next most beautiful creatures of all. They are soft, furry, cuddly, and blindingly trusting. In addition to proper nutrition, exercise, and veterinary care, kittens need attention—lots of it. Some of the best quality time spent with your kitten will be doing Cat Massage. Create your own style of Kitten Massage. Your pre-cat will love you for it!

Extra patience and effort will reap huge rewards as you modify techniques for your kitten's delicate size. Kittens are so frisky and playful that you may find it harder to use long, slow strokes. Using four fingers together, and a full palm can be too much, so use more finger pads and one or two fingers together. Be very careful with longer fingernails, since kittens move so quickly. Motions are generally the same, just smaller and slower. Obviously, pressure is much lighter. No deep work! Although some Kitten Massages will be gentle and relaxed, most will be playful and frolicky fun.

In the human kingdom, children have wonderful qualities similar to kittens. (Not as furry, perhaps, but just as cuddly.) One of the best advantages a growing child can have is the affection, friendship, and responsibility that comes with a cat. I've stressed the importance and value of cat-human bonding throughout this book. This translates into child-parent bonding as well. Cat Massage sessions provide perfect opportunities to spend quality time with your child. Pay special attention to the approach and feedback, always making sure that both cat and child are equally comfortable. If either becomes uncomfortable, do not force the issue—take a break, and resume Cat Massage again later. Start with very short introductory sessions. It may take a while for your cat not to run away from small hands, or for your child not to be afraid of the cat. It's also best for your cat to be seated—not held—during training times (mega ouch!), and preferably seated on an equal level or slightly above your child, for their comfort. Proceed slowly and calmly through the steps, explaining parts of the hand, and how to use them. With kittens, modify techniques for your child. Pick one or two strokes for them to gain expertise with before continuing. Make sure you watch them closely and guide their hands for appropriate stroking. Keep the speed slow and the pressure featherlight. *Never* leave your cat and child alone together until your child understands how to touch a cat, and your cat is comfortable with your child's hand. Be prepared: it can be a very patient and time-consuming process, but the benefits outweigh the efforts. Your child will feel a real accomplishment when your cat walks past you and approaches your child for a massage.

Teach them everything you've learned about Cat Massage very slowly, teach them patiently, and most of all, teach them with love. Then let them teach you. Experience Cat Massage through a child's eyes. Your child will delight in a new world of fun, will learn the art of gentleness, and your feline friend will be grateful for another tender touch.

The Wisdom of Age: Senior Stroking

Senior citizens are the wisest of all of us. Whether four-legged or two-legged, they deserve every major and minor consideration possible. Even the most arthritic hands can Cat Massage, and even the most aging feline will welcome that caress. Most speeds, understandably, will be slower and moods gentle and relaxed. Nobody, whether cat or human, is too old for touch. Studies in nursing homes prove how necessary and valuable touch is for our elderly people. If studies were done among the older cat population, no doubt the same facts would hold true.

Older Cats need to be given consideration and understanding for their age. They may not react as quickly as a kitten, or be as cute as a kitten, but just like our elderly people, they have a special beauty and joy reserved for their special age. It may not be as obvious or playful as that of a kitten, but look for it, it's there. Treat them with kindness and patience. They deserve it.

Let's Mention Mommy: Pregnant Cats

Pregnant cats and new mommies can benefit from all that Cat Massage offers. Good prenatal care includes Cat Massage for Mommy; always check with your veterinarian to guide your massages through her pregnancy, especially as birth time approaches. She will surely welcome your soothing touch during this time. Her kittens will have experienced the gifts of massage even before they're born. Avoid abdominal and belly work, except for the lightest stroking. Perhaps she will need deeper work on her shoulders, arms, and legs to compensate for her extra weight. Techniques can stay the same for the head, neck, paws and claws, and tail—just slower and softer. Throughout her pregnancy, patiently allow for any personality changes that may include a desire for more massage or no massage. She may even have changes in her temperment. Just be there for her. Whether she expresses it or not, your support is absolutely needed and appreciated. After delivery, she'll let you know when she's ready to resume full Cat Massage workouts.

Ailing and Recuperating: Cats and People

An injured animal instinctively licks and rubs a hurt area, just as a mother lovingly strokes her sick child. When we are sick, there's nothing like a soothing touch to help us feel better. It's the best medicine.

Never massage an inflamed area or one where your cat reacts in pain. If there is any question about your cat's health, bring her to a veterinarian. Take the extra knowledge you've gained about your cat's condition from your massage to her doctor for proper diagnosis. If your cat is injured, proper veterinary care is needed. There may be medical reasons to wait before continuing Cat Massage. Always consult with your veterinarian to make sure you are helping—not further injuring your cat. With a terminally ill cat, under veterinary guidelines, Cat Massage can offer soothing relief.

For population control and health concerns, all cats should be spayed or neutered. After this procedure, as with any surgery, ask your vet how soon you can resume Cat Massage. Although you won't be directly massaging the affected site, massaging other areas can help the recovery process.

People who are ailing may find great comfort in their cat's attention or even mere presence. Some cats instinctively sense if you are sick and do their best to curl up with you and purr you back to health. From a simple case of the blues, a cold, or being flat on your back, the companionship of your cat is invaluable.

Cat and human alike, we all welcome the healing power of massage, because it truly is therapeutic touch.